WATER POLLUTION

WATER POLLUTION

KATHLYN GAY

Franklin Watts
New York/London/Toronto/Sydney
*An Impact Book/*1990

*To all those who are working to save our water
and other natural resources*

Diagrams by Vantage Art

Photographs courtesy of: A. F. Amos: p. 2; U.S. Geological Survey:
pp. 26 (D. R. LeBlanc), 68 (D. A. Rickert); Center for Marine
Conservation: pp. 90 (John Domont/Marine Debris Information Center),
93 (Ron Heron/N.M.F.S.-M.S.).
Remaining photographs are courtesy of the author.

Library of Congress Cataloging-in-Publication Data

Gay, Kathlyn.
    Water pollution / Kathlyn Gay.
        p. cm. — (An Impact Book)
    Includes bibliographical references and index.
    Summary: Discuss the problem of our contaminated rivers, lakes.
and oceans and proposes ways to purify them.
    ISBN 0-531-10949-6
    1. Water—Pollution—United States—Juvenile literature. 2. Water
quality management—United States—Juvenile literature. [1. Water—
Pollution. 2. Water quality management.] I. Title.
TD223.G38 1990
363.73'94'0973—dc20   90-37496 CIP AC

CONTENTS

CHAPTER ONE
DECADES OF DIRTY WATER 9

Water Resources/10   The Hydrologic Cycle/11
Unequal Distribution/13   What Pollutes the
Water?/14   Some Improvements/17

CHAPTER TWO
THREATS TO GROUNDWATER 19

How an Aquifer Is Contaminated/20
Danger from Sewage/23   Industrial Wastes/25
Dangerous Landfills and Dumps/29   Agricultural
Contaminants/30   Urban Pollutants/33
Another Threat—Overdrafts/35

CHAPTER THREE
WASTE WATER PROBLEMS 37

Waste Water Disposal/38   Treating Waste
Water/40   Reclaiming and Recyling Water/42
Other Reclamation Projects/43

CHAPTER FOUR
VITAL LINKS—WETLANDS 46

Where Are Wetlands?/48 Why Save a Swamp
(or Other Wetland)?/49 Causes of Wetland
Losses/52 Conservation and Management/54

CHAPTER FIVE
SCUM GREEN AND ICE BLUE LAKES 60

Small Lakes, Big Problems/61 Save Our Lake
Revisited/65 Ice Blue Acidic Lakes/70

CHAPTER SIX
TROUBLE IN RIVER CITY 74

Water Quality—Good and Bad News/75
The PCB Connection/77
More Sources of Pollution/80
Changing in Midstream/81

CHAPTER SEVEN
SEAS OF DEBRIS 84

Don't Go Near the Water—or Beach/86 Ties
That Bind and Kill/89 Awash in Oil/95
The Global Sewer/98

CHAPTER EIGHT
WHEN WELLS, RIVERS, AND
LAKES GO DRY 102

Managing Water Resources/103 Stretching
Water Resources/104
Obstacles to Conservation/108

CHAPTER NINE
PROTECTIVE MEASURES 112

Environmental Laws/113 Cooperative Efforts/117
"Attack Bugs" and Other Cleanup Methods/119
Controlling Industrial Toxins/121 Educational
Programs/122

CHAPTER TEN
TAKING ACTION 125

Should You Drink the Water?/125
Stewardship/127

Agencies and Organizations/130
Source Notes/132 Glossary/136 For Further
Reading/138 Index/141

CHAPTER ONE
DECADES OF DIRTY WATER

SAVE OUR LAKE. The title line for the booklet was printed across a cover photograph of the sparkling, blue-green waters of Lake Michigan. But superimposed over the water was a close-up of a large hand covered and dripping with slime and muck. Most people looking at the illustration would react with a disgusted "Yuk!," which is clearly what the *Chicago Tribune* editorial staff expected. They had prepared the booklet during the 1960s, compiling many news stories that called attention to the increasingly serious problem of pollution in Lake Michigan, as well as other Great Lakes.

Related and contributing problems involved polluted rivers that drained into the Great Lakes as well as bays and oceans from coast to coast. Rivers, coated with oil and grease, had become contaminated with human wastes, all kinds of debris, and *toxic* chemicals from industries.

State and federal laws were passed in the 1970s to ban certain pollutants that threatened water resources, and the quality of many lakes and rivers began to improve. However, contaminants continued to degrade some waterways, and water pollution is still a major public concern in the United States and also in other industrialized nations. Pollution compounds another problem. As world population continues to increase, it becomes ever more difficult to meet the great demand for potable (drinkable) water and to supply the water needs of agriculture, industry, and energy production.

WATER RESOURCES

Our earth sometimes has been called a water planet, since its surface is more than 70 percent water. An estimated 97 percent of the total world supply of water is in the oceans. Ocean water contains dissolved mineral salts that have washed from the land and have accumulated over millions of years. Although organisms need salt for life, the high *salinity*, or salt content, of seawater makes it unsuitable for drinking and agriculture. The human body and most crops need fresh water—that is, water with low concentrations of salt.

About 3 percent of the planet's supply of water is fresh, but most of that is tied up in glaciers and ice caps at the North and South Poles. Scientists estimate that only about 0.3 percent of the world's fresh water supply is available for drinking and agricultural purposes. Nevertheless, that supply is immense. It comes from streams, rivers, lakes, and underground sources called *aquifers*, which vary in size, soil type, and rock formations.

Contrary to popular belief, an aquifer is not a large underground river, lake, or pool. Water in an aquifer is stored in porous rocks like sandstone or in rock fractures and in the tiny spaces, called pores, between soil particles. A layer of impermeable rock—solid rock that does not allow the water to seep through—usually lies beneath an aquifer or surrounds it. The water in the aquifer is replenished by rain, snow, and other precipitation. In some aquifers, pressure from water at higher levels in the aquifer forces water to the surface in a spring. But in most cases, people have to dig wells to tap the water in aquifers.

THE HYDROLOGIC CYCLE

Huge amounts of fresh water are constantly being used each day, but the total worldwide supply remains fairly constant—about a million cubic miles (4,300,000 cu km).[1] Fresh water on the planet does not disappear. It is a renewable resource, constantly changing forms as it moves through a never-ending cycle called the "hydrologic cycle." The hydrologic, or water, cycle includes three major processes: evaporation, condensation, and precipitation.

If you get out of a pool or come from a swim in a lake or river on a hot day, you know that water on your body seems to disappear soon after being exposed to the sun and air. Heat causes the water droplets to evaporate, or change to a vapor.

The heat of the sun evaporates water from the surface of the oceans—about 80,000 cubic miles (330,000 cu km) each year. Water also evaporates from rivers, streams, lakes, ponds, pools, and other bodies of water. Evaporation takes place as well from the leaves of plants in a process called *evapotranspiration*.

During the hydrologic cycle (see Figure 1), water vapor sometimes condenses to form clouds, or changes into liquid, or freezes, forming crystals. In other words it becomes dew, rain, snow, sleet, or hail, most of which falls into the seas. Winds sweep

[11]

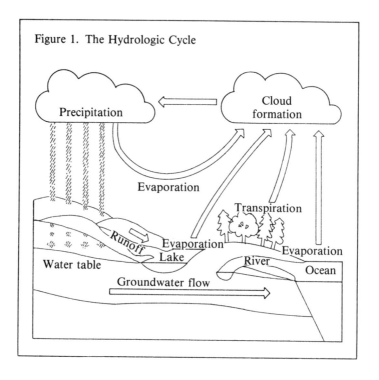

Figure 1. The Hydrologic Cycle

some precipitation inland, where it mixes with water vapor from the land. Clouds form and precipitation falls to replenish such freshwater sources as rivers, lakes, and groundwater.

All the precipitation that falls on land eventually returns to the sea, although that process could take thousands of years if moisture is locked in polar ice caps or in slow-moving groundwater. Much of the fresh water that flows back to the oceans does so by surface runoffs that end up in streams and rivers, which empty into the seas. At the same time, surface water continues to evaporate, and condensation and precipitation take place over and over again.

[12]

UNEQUAL DISTRIBUTION

Although the water cycle has no beginning or end, there are limits to the way water is distributed and who has access to the fresh water on the planet. According to a research professor in the Chemistry Department of American University, the United States, "based upon its size, is blessed with five times her share (proportionately) of the world's non-salt and usable waters," but uses seven times the amount of water consumed by people in arid countries.[2]

A report from the U.S. Department of Agriculture (USDA) shows that Americans withdraw at least 309 billion gallons per day (bgd) of fresh water from ground- and surface water sources. Another 72 bgd are withdrawn from the oceans for industrial use. Much of the fresh water is consumptively used, which means the water evaporates or is incorporated in plants or animals or manufactured products, and thus cannot be reused immediately. On the other hand, all but 2 bgd of ocean water goes back to seas or estuaries—bays and lagoons where salt water and fresh water mix.[3]

The high rate of water consumption has created shortages in some parts of the nation. The demand for water in the rapidly growing cities of the Southwest, for example, exceeds the renewable supply. In fact, for decades people in desert and semiarid regions of the United States have built dams and reservoirs, constructed canals and irrigation systems, and passed laws that would help bring water to the parched land and supply the daily needs of the increasing populations.

Throughout American history and for that matter throughout human history, people have fought and sometimes died for the right to a particular supply of fresh water. Major cities have grown up along waterways, not only because of the human need for water but also because waterways are an important means of transportation and a source of electric power so vital to the development of industries and businesses. Yet such activities have polluted water resources.

During the 1980s, the U.S. Environmental Protection Agency (EPA) asked the states to report their major concerns about water quality. Some of the reported problems are national in scope and include contaminated groundwater and polluted surface waters such as rivers, streams, and lakes. The loss of wetlands and toxic pollutants in coastal waters and estuaries also are major problems.[4]

WHAT POLLUTES THE WATER?

How do pollutants contaminate the waters? When is the quality of water impaired? To answer these questions, hydrologists (water experts) first have to determine how water is being used. Irrigation water, for example, does not have to be the same quality as drinking water. Water is tested for a specific purpose and if found to be of poor quality for that purpose, then the experts must determine what the pollutants are and how they interact with the environment to harm water supplies. The source or sources of pollutants also must be identified.

In some cases, pollutants may come from a pipe discharging into a river, from a boat, irrigation ditch, underground storage tank, or other single source, called a "point source" of pollution. But frequently there are varied sources, collectively called a "nonpoint source," that could include pollutants from industries, agriculture, and other human activities.

Some of the major contaminants since the 1940s have been phosphorus and nitrogen. These so-called conventional pollutants are actually natural elements that plants and animals need for growth. If there is an abundant supply of phosphorus and nitrogen in water, *algae* and other aquatic plants grow rapidly. At times, algae develop for several miles. A body of water or a waterway then may become "eutrophic," a term that biologists use to describe a well-nourished lake or stream. When there is an excessive amount of nutrients, the water is said to be "hypereutrophic."

The rapidly growing plants in water also decay quickly, and in the process they use up the oxygen supply. As a result, fish and other aquatic life die.

During the 1960s many U.S. lakes and streams were being overnourished with phosphorus that came from detergents—washing compounds. Eventually detergents with phosphorus were restricted, but nutrients from fertilizers and untreated sewage flowing through municipal waste-disposal plants added to the problem.

One body of water that suffered from *eutrophication* was Lake Erie. William Ashworth, who has written extensively on water pollution problems, described how algae choked portions of the lake: "Hundreds of square miles of it formed great mats up to two feet [0.6 m] thick on the Lake's surface; pieces of the mats thousands of acres in size broke free and washed up on the beaches. Water intakes were fouled; drinking-water supplies took on the distinctive, disgusting taste of rotting vegetation."[5]

Nutrient overloads were not the only pollution problems. Lake beaches often were closed because of high counts of fecal coliform bacteria from raw sewage—human waste—that flowed into rivers and streams emptying into lakes. Although coliform bacteria are not harmful themselves, they usually indicate that *pathogens*, disease-causing organisms, are present.

Many rivers in the nation also were polluted, usually with industrial wastes. The Cuyahoga River, which runs through Cleveland and empties into Lake Erie, was an infamous case. News reports during 1952–53 pointed out that every day at least 155 tons of chemicals, metals, oils, and salts were dumped directly into the Cuyahoga. The pollutants came from such industries as meat packers, oil refineries, steel plants, paint companies, and tar distilleries.

The river was not only foul-smelling and full of ugly debris, but also highly flammable. Concentrations of methane gas and oil slicks caused the river surface to catch fire on several occasions. One spectacular blaze in 1969 burned over several miles through a murky industrial section of Cleveland. The fire finally convinced authorities at the local, state, and federal levels that action had to be taken to clean up not only the Cuyahoga but also other tributaries that feed into the Great Lakes.

Smaller amounts of biological pollutants and fewer industrial wastes flow into the Great Lakes today, and water quality has improved somewhat. But other pollution problems have developed and nutrient overload is a serious threat to other lakes in the nation and also to coastal areas. In addition, some freshwater resources are endangered by heavy metals and toxins from industry, drainage from cities, farms, and waste disposal sites. Salts—inorganic and organic—pollute some water supplies in the nation, as do soil sediments that may carry harmful pesticides and bacteria. Acid deposition—

that is, wet and dry deposits of *acidic* particles that come from industrial and motor vehicle emissions— is another type of pollutant that endangers freshwater sources.

SOME IMPROVEMENTS

As the public became more aware of water pollution problems during the 1960s, many groups and individuals began to demand action. Over the next decade, Congress passed laws designed to protect water supplies and to control pollutants from industries and businesses. During the 1980s, a number of federal regulations were strengthened, in spite of vetoes by former president Ronald Reagan, whose administration was dedicated to deregulation. But Americans wanted more stringent control over water quality, and Congress placed additional bans on pollutants and increased funds to protect fresh water supplies.

In early 1987, *U.S. News & World Report* noted that

the quality of some 47,000 miles [75,600 km] of monitored streams is markedly improved. In Lake Erie—pronounced biologically dead 15 years ago—perch, walleye and even largemouth bass and coho salmon are thriving. Trout have returned to the Hudson River near New York City.

But elsewhere, 311,000 miles, [500,500 km] of water have worsened or remain unchanged. Industrial poisons . . . have turned Boston Harbor into a murky soup from which people haul flounder with large liver tumors and cancerous sores. . . . [6]

[17]

As for the quality of drinking water, "More Americans are receiving safer drinking water than ever before," an editorial report in the *EPA Journal* stated in late 1988. However, the Environmental Protection Agency (EPA) also pointed out that there are still many troublesome contaminants, including lead and radioactive materials, especially "in small community [water] systems, which have a low level of compliance with national drinking water standards."[7]

The EPA also is concerned about protection of groundwater, which is being contaminated by a number of pollutants. Groundwater is a source of drinking water for nearly half of the U.S. population, including 97 percent of all rural residents. It is also used for irrigation and plays an essential role in replenishing surface waters and nourishing many ecosystems.

CHAPTER TWO
THREATS TO
GROUNDWATER

In recent years, many government agencies and environmental groups have expressed concern about the quality of groundwater. But just what is this essential resource? How is water stored and replenished in aquifers? How do pollutants move into the water supply?

Most aquifers—known as unconfined aquifers—soak up water, somewhat like a sponge, until no more can be absorbed in the soil. The top of this saturated strata of soil is usually referred to as the water table. That boundary level changes as water is drawn off by well pumps or seeps into streams. The water table also changes as the aquifer is replenished by precipitation, and by runoff from the land and surface waters.

Another type of aquifer is known as a confined aquifer. It traps water between solid rock or soils such as clay and might sit below or beside an unconfined aquifer. Because of the geologic pressure, water from the confined aquifer may not need to be pumped but may flow to the surface on its own—as it does in a spring.

An aquifer may be close to the surface or deep

below ground level. It can range in thickness from a few to several hundred feet, spreading over a small area or up to hundreds of square miles.

Vast stores of water sit in aquifers across the United States. The amount of groundwater within a half mile (0.8 km) of the land surface of the conterminous United States (those forty-eight states within the same national boundary) is enough to fill Lake Michigan thirty-three times, according to a USDA analysis. Much more groundwater lies at deeper levels, but it is usually too saline for human consumption. Although not all groundwater is accessible, the amount "that can be retrieved with current technologies is at least six times greater than all the water stored in our surface lakes and reservoirs," the Conservation Foundation reported.[8]

Just as aquifers vary in size and geologic formation, so they also vary in the rate of water movement. Water flow is determined by the geologic material in the aquifer and by gravity. Sometimes the movement is artificially changed because of pumping from wells, but the natural flow might range from a few feet to several thousand feet per year.

HOW AN AQUIFER
IS CONTAMINATED

Water flow and geologic materials have a direct bearing on groundwater contamination. If poisonous materials seep into an aquifer that is fast-moving, the *toxic plume*, as it is called, will spread quickly and may contaminate an entire aquifer before any corrective measures can be taken. Even in a slow-moving aquifer, pollutants can cause serious problems. A plume may not be discovered for many years. By then it may be too late to save the aquifer, and the sources of contamination may be very difficult to identify.

Until recently it had been generally accepted that soils would filter out contaminants before they reached an aquifer, and that water supplies would thus be protected. Certainly some geologic materials will absorb, or take up, various substances. Or soils may adsorb toxic substances. In simple terms, *adsorption* means that chemicals (such as those in pesticides) are attracted to the surface of some solid materials. If adsorption takes place, pollutants may travel with soil particles to a body of water or detach from a surface and move down through the soil into an aquifer. The downward movement of water or other liquids through the soil is known as *percolation*.

The vegetation and bacteria in some soils will neutralize some contaminants, and clay can slow the progress of various pollutants through the soil. The location of an aquifer—whether it is shallow or deep under ground—also determines whether it can be easily polluted.

Another factor in groundwater contamination is the amount of pollutants. A sudden leak or spill from a tank of gasoline, for example, could overload the soil's capacity to filter substances that might pollute groundwater. Figure 2 illustrates how various pollutants may contaminate aquifers.

Some groundwater sources are unaffected by human activities, but that does not necessarily mean the water is "pure." As water seeps through the soil to aquifers it dissolves minerals in rocks. Naturally occurring elements in water include iron, sodium, magnesium, potassium, and calcium, which are not usually a threat to human health. Minerals in water often give it a pleasant taste or provide a natural

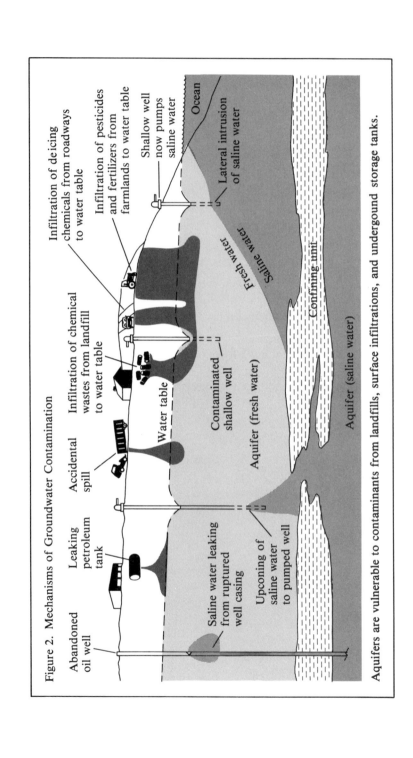

Figure 2. Mechanisms of Groundwater Contamination

Abandoned oil well

Leaking petroleum tank

Accidental spill

Infiltration of chemical wastes from landfill to water table

Infiltration of de-icing chemicals from roadways to water table

Infiltration of pesticides and fertilizers from farmlands to water table

Shallow well now pumps saline water

Ocean

Lateral intrusion of saline water

Fresh water

Saline water

Confining unit

Aquifer (saline water)

Aquifer (fresh water)

Contaminated shallow well

Water table

Upconing of saline water to pumped well

Saline water leaking from ruptured well casing

Aquifers are vulnerable to contaminants from landfills, surface infiltrations, and undergound storage tanks.

effervescence or bubbling. In fact, natural mineral water has become a popular bottled beverage in the United States, Canada, and many European countries.

Yet some natural elements in water supplies can be harmful. High levels of iron in water, for example, can be acidic and corrode pipes and other materials. Radon, a poisonous gas that forms from the decay of uranium ore found in rock formations in various parts of the United States, has been discovered in groundwater supplies of a number of states.

Nitrates, too, may occur in high enough levels in groundwater to be dangerous to health. Nitrates are formed from nitrogen that has become oxidized, and come from the breakdown of vegetation and also from deposits of soil and rock. However, high levels of nitrates in groundwater usually come from fertilizer residues, animal wastes, and landfills. Nitrates in drinking water can cause what is known as "blue-baby syndrome," a reaction among infants that cuts off oxygen to the brain. Nitrates may also be responsible for some cancers. One Australian study linked birth defects to nitrates in drinking water consumed by women during pregnancy.[9]

DANGER FROM SEWAGE

Human waste and toxic chemicals dumped into sewage systems are "probably the greatest threats to groundwater quality and human health," according to the Conservation Foundation.[10] Of particular concern are on-site sewage disposal systems—septic tanks, cesspools, and outhouses. About 20 million are in use, primarily in the rural areas of at least thirty-six states. Pathogens, or disease-causing biological organisms such as viruses and bacteria, may escape from septic systems through a process known as *leaching* and seep through soil to groundwater.

During the 1700s and 1800s many thousands of people throughout the world suffered from diseases such as cholera, typhoid, and diphtheria caused by biological contaminants in well water and in lakes and streams. Even today an estimated 25,000 people worldwide die of waterborne diseases.[11] But organisms that endanger health and life can be destroyed with the use of chlorine, a disinfectant, in water. However, too much chlorine can also be hazardous to health, and chlorine has no effect on many synthetic chemical compounds. The boiling of water and the use of filtering systems also help to remove harmful biological agents from well water.

Although bacteria decompose solid wastes or the wastes are removed from most septic systems, up to one-third of the on-site waste systems in the nation do not operate properly. Many of these allow an excess of nitrates to contaminate water supplies. One study by the U.S. Geological Survey (USGS) found that 20 percent of a sampling of 124,000 wells across the nation exceeded EPA's nitrate level of 3 milligrams per liter (mg/l). Wells tested in at least six states had nitrate levels over 10 mg/l.[12]

Toxic substances that have been poured down drains or that seep into groundwater from septic tanks can be health hazards also. Other contaminants include septic tank cleaners that contain such hazardous chemicals as trichloroethylene (TCE), known to cause cancer in animals.

How can this source of contamination be controlled? Some experts have recommended that one of the primary protective measures is proper maintenance and cleaning of septic tanks, which would help eliminate the need for chemical cleaners. Another measure is repairing or replacing systems in which pipes or tanks have corroded or been damaged.

Location of septic systems is also important. There should not be a high concentration of septic systems in any area, and they should not be placed in areas where contaminants can move quickly through the soil into drinking water wells or to an aquifer, experts say.

INDUSTRIAL WASTES

In 1984, a florist in the southwestern Michigan village of Edwardsburg complained to the state public health department that house plants kept in the shop were dying from the water. Tests confirmed that the well water being used was contaminated with several toxic chemicals. Since that time, specialists with the Michigan Department of Natural Resources (MDNR) have been testing dozens of wells in the village as well as in other parts of the state. The specialists have found high levels of toxins in the groundwater of some communities, including *tetrachlorethylene*, a cleaning solvent, and benzene, *toluene,* and *xylene*, which are usually associated with petroleum products.

Since the toxins were discovered in the small Michigan village, homes and businesses that once depended on well water have been connected to the public water system, which is considered safe. But even though people were not using the contaminated well water, efforts began in late 1987 to clean up the pollutants. As one official from the MDNR put it: "This stuff doesn't just sit there. It moves."

At the time the contaminants were discovered

Sludge-drying beds and sand beds surround a sewage treatment plant in Massachusetts, as shown in this aerial photo.

they were in a sandy aquifer close to the surface, but were expected to seep through cracks in clay and gravel to a lower aquifer. The plume of toxins has been moving away from the well that supplies the public water system, but officials fear the chemicals could contaminate other wells far from the village.

Where did the chemicals come from? According to the MDNR specialists, a variety of businesses may be to blame, including a dry cleaner, a plastics company, a paint shop, and a gas station. Plumes of chemicals were found radiating from these businesses. But since this discovery, there has been debate over which companies, if any, should be responsible for cleaning up the groundwater contaminants.

A similar situation, but on a larger scale, exists in a fast-growing residential area near South Bend, Indiana. Storage tanks for the petroleum company Amoco are located in the area, and during the 1970s there were several major spills from the "tank farm." The spills have contaminated groundwater with 1,2 dichloroethane (1,2 DCA), used in degreasers and in leaded gasoline, which Amoco distributed from its tanks until 1986. Several other solvents from the tanks have also been found in water samples. Environmental Protection Agency officials say that the plume of contaminated groundwater from the tank farm is moving toward a new housing development and could affect wells in the area by the mid-1990s.

Spills are not the only way that pollutants seep into aquifers. The chemical and petroleum industries have used injection wells since the 1950s to dispose of wastes. These wells usually are between 3,000 and 12,000 feet (900 and 3,700 m) deep. Sitting far below an aquifer that supplies potable groundwater, the wells handle deposits of brine (water full of salt) from oil and gas industries, toxic chemicals, and radioactive wastes.

Theoretically, properly designed and placed injection wells can hold contaminants safely forever. But wells placed over aquifers or corroded wells can allow toxic substances to seep into potable water. Leaks from injection wells have contaminated underground drinking water supplies in a number of states, including Pennsylvania, Ohio, Illinois, Louisiana, and Texas.

Underground storage tanks are another source of aquifer contamination. Gas stations, airports, and similar facilities store a high volume of petroleum products in underground tanks; above ground the materials could be fire hazards. Industries that use or manufacture toxic chemicals also store potentially dangerous substances in underground tanks. According to one congressional research report, nationwide there could be up to 10 million underground tanks, storing fluids ranging from fuel to solvents.

Unfortunately, most underground tanks are made of steel and may begin to corrode after fifteen to twenty years. Several million of these tanks have been underground since the 1970s. Having reached the end of their expected lifespan, many tanks could be leaking toxic materials.

As an example, the EPA surveyed underground tanks in a northern California area called Silicon Valley, where many electronic industries are located. The industries use underground tanks to store solvents for cleaning computer chips. Of the ninety-six tanks surveyed, seventy-five were leaking and were contaminating soil or groundwater.

Even underground tanks made of fiber glass,

which is noncorrosive, can leak if they are damaged when installed. Pipes leading to tanks can corrode and leak, and there is always the danger of spills as tanks are filled or emptied. Although the EPA estimates that about 1.5 million underground tanks contain hazardous materials, there is no clear picture on how many underground steel or fiber glass tanks pose a threat to groundwater supplies. Not all tanks presently in use have been registered with state environmental agencies, which would help identify the liquids stored underground. Also, many underground storage tanks have been abandoned and could be an unsuspected source of groundwater contamination.

DANGEROUS LANDFILLS
AND DUMPS

Love Canal has become a sad chapter in U.S. environmental history, symbolizing the hazards of toxic waste. During the 1940s, the abandoned canal near Niagara Falls was thought to be the perfect place to dispose of wastes from a nearby chemical plant. Dump the chemicals in the canal, cover them over with dirt, and the hazardous substances could no longer pose a threat to human health, right? Not so, as people in the area learned years later when many became ill and trees and shrubs began to die.

People living near Love Canal were evacuated, and laws have been passed to regulate disposal of hazardous wastes, substances considered a threat to public health or the environment. As a result, some waste disposal sites have been lined with plastic or rubber sheeting or have been located on impermeable soil such as clay to prevent seepage of toxic materials into groundwater.

Yet nationwide there still are many disposal sites that could be sources of groundwater contamination. An example is surface impoundments—the pits, lagoons, ponds, and other holding areas for both hazardous and nonhazardous municipal and industrial wastes. Of the 180,000 such sites in the United States, many were established before there was widespread knowledge about the dangers to groundwater. The impoundments were located over usable aquifers, which today makes them a serious threat to potable water.

According to the EPA, there are also an estimated 93,000 landfills that cities and industries nationwide once used to dispose of household and industrial waste not considered hazardous. But some of those waste sites are polluting, or have the potential to contaminate, groundwater with pathogens. The EPA has also identified about 19,000 abandoned and uncontrolled hazardous waste sites nationwide. At least 4,000 of these sites are responsible for some groundwater contamination.[13]

Of course the problem is not confined to the United States. In West Germany, for example, at least 10 percent of the drinking water supplies are contaminated with fertilizers. High amounts of pesticides have been detected in Italy's drinking water.[14] Industries worldwide have long used surface waters—rivers, streams, lakes, swamps, and ponds—as dumping sites for their wastes. These are the sources of many toxic substances that seep into soils and eventually aquifers.

AGRICULTURAL CONTAMINANTS

Chemical fertilizers to increase crop production, chemical pesticides to kill insects that prey on crops, chemical herbicides to kill weeds, and chemical fungicides to destroy mold and rot in growing plants and stored seed—all are part of modern agriculture in industrialized nations. In what some have called an "agrochemical addiction," millions of tons of these substances are used in commercial farming, and the volume has increased rapidly since the 1970s.[15]

Synthetic chemicals have been extremely effective in agriculture. Fertilizers, for example, have helped to more than double production of crops such as corn. But as environmentalists and some government agencies have pointed out, some farmers use much more fertilizer than their crops need. The residue may pollute a watershed, an area of land where the groundwater and runoff from storms or irrigation empty into the same body of water such as a river or lake.

Some types of fertilizers are basically potash or phosphate, which soils do not easily adsorb, so there is little threat to groundwater. But half of all artificial fertilizers used contain nitrogen, and with heavy use nitrates build up in soils, percolate to aquifers, and contaminate drinking water.

The pesticides, herbicides, and fungicides—poisons that kill pests, weeds, molds, and so on—also have been overused and are creating hazards to the environment and to public health. Certainly pesticides are effective in killing insect pests and thus protect crops that the insects may ravage. But at the same time pesticides could be destroying other life, such as the insect predators that naturally feed on insect pests and the birds that eat insects whose bodies contain pesticides. In addition, large volumes of agricultural poisons end up in the soil and percolate into aquifers. From East Coast farms to West Coast orchards, from midwestern cornfields to southern farmlands, abuse of agricultural chemicals has resulted in drinking water laced with poisons.

In recent years, many farmers and ranchers have begun efforts to control substances that could pollute groundwater. The U.S. Department of Agriculture announced in 1988 that one of its top priorities would be "protection of water quality from agricultural and other rural nonpoint sources of contamination." In a ten-year (1988–1997) National Program for Soil and Water Conservation, the USDA has begun to work with states and local communities. States have the authority to set water quality standards, but the USDA is emphasizing research and education, and assisting with management techniques to deal with agricultural chemicals, water conservation, pest control, and organic waste (animal manure) disposal.

Yet some farmers and ranchers resist legal means to control agricultural practices. In California's San Joaquin Valley, for example, farmers have been protesting the state's tough new restrictions on pesticide residues on food. Growers also have argued against new controls on chemicals in farm runoff, water from irrigation that is discharged into surface waters or seeps into groundwater.

Much of the farm runoff in the San Joaquin Valley contains the metal selenium. The metal, which occurs naturally in rock formations, is flushed out of the rocks by the irrigation water. Selenium has caused reproductive damage in birds whose habitat is the nearby wetlands. But one grower summed up the general attitude of many farmers when he asked: "Are a few dozen birds more important to preserve than irrigated agriculture?"

Those in favor of stiffer regulations against pollutants would respond that both wildlife and agriculture are important to save. In addition, selenium and other chemicals in agricultural runoff threaten human health and life.

URBAN POLLUTANTS

After a rainstorm or during a thaw of snow and ice in cities and towns, water may leak or overflow from storm sewer pipes, and the street runoff can then percolate into the ground. Urban runoff may carry metals such as cadmium, copper, and lead as well as toxic compounds such as cyanide and some pesticides. Organic pollutants such as animal droppings also have been found in urban runoff.

A variety of urban activities can lead to groundwater contamination. Hazardous chemicals used by businesses, such as cleaning solvents or petroleum products, may be dumped on the ground. In construction, toxic waterproofing chemicals and fuels from heavy equipment can contaminate soil and groundwater. Herbicides to control weeds along highways and oil or other materials spread on roads to control dust are other potential pollutants.

Deicing salt is one more major contaminant in urban runoff. In the "snow-belt" states, street crews spread salt to melt snow and ice on local and state roadways, and salty meltwater seeps into groundwater and wetlands. At least $300 million is spent annually on deicing salts for the nation's roads, but the damages to water resources as well as roads and bridges runs into the billions of dollars.

Excess salt in lakes may destroy young fish and other aquatic life. Salt also contaminates private wells, forcing people to find other sources of water.

Although no city in the snow-belt area has banned the use of deicing salt, "one has been able to keep

[33]

Drainage from city streets may not look polluted, but toxic compounds in urban runoff can contaminate groundwater and waterways.

itself on a low-salt diet," according to a *National Wildlife* report. That city, Madison, Wisconsin, now uses a salt-and-sand mixture for its major roads and only sand on other streets. During the winter of 1986–87, the city was able to reduce its use of salt by 42 percent as measured against a comparable winter in the 1970s.[16]

ANOTHER THREAT—OVERDRAFTS

Even when an aquifer is fairly well protected, it can be threatened by overuse. Large withdrawals from a single aquifer can alter the flow of groundwater and change the location of recharge areas, lowering the level of streams and lakes, which can deplete the groundwater further.

Excessive withdrawals, or overdrafts, also lead to subsidence. As the aquifer compacts, the earth sinks, and tens of millions of dollars in damages may result. Damages from sinking land in the San Joaquin Valley, California, have totaled at least $100 million. In one area, land has subsided nearly 30 feet (over 9 m) over several decades.[17]

In coastal areas, an overdrafted aquifer may fill with salt water, making it unfit for agriculture and human consumption. Salt water has intruded into aquifers and also some canals of south Florida. Similar problems exist along the Gulf of Mexico in Louisiana and Texas.

Another example is California's Oxnard Plain. Area farmers have pumped more fresh water from under this plain than has been replaced by rainfall. As a result, the water table (the level below which the ground is saturated with water) has dropped, and seawater has seeped in to replace the fresh water.

Only the top layer of the aquifer has seawater,

according to county officials, who plan to correct the problem. A pipeline was built to bring irrigation water from other sources to farmers in the Oxnard Plain. By using this water for irrigation, pumping from the overdrafted aquifer has been reduced. The aquifer will be recharged naturally and by artificial means, such as pumping water into the aquifer, but the process could take many years.

CHAPTER THREE
WASTE WATER
PROBLEMS

Taking a shower, washing dishes or clothes, flushing the toilet, pouring cleaning water down the drain—many times a day people generate waste water in their homes. Each household in the United States uses about 230 gallons (870 liters) of water daily.[18] This does not include indirect use of water through consumer goods and services. In manufacturing, water is needed for cooling, washing away impurities, and many other purposes. The food industry uses water for processing and preserving. All of the used water becomes waste water that must be disposed of in some way.

In urban areas, much of the waste water from homes, businesses, and industries flows from buildings through underground pipelines to sewage treatment plants. But many sewer systems in fast-growing cities or in older metropolitan areas are unable to adequately handle the vast amount of waste water that flows through them.

We are "Swamped by Our Own Sewage,"[19] the title of one magazine article declared, and it certainly seems that way with reports of human fecal matter on beaches and brown slicks of raw sewage in bays and rivers. In many crowded urban centers such as New York and Chicago, sewer systems collect storm water as well as other waste water. At one time, this was not a problem since rain or snow melts soaked into open land areas. Now, however, roads, parking lots, sidewalks, and buildings cover much of the land, and storm water and melting snow flow into street drains and on into sewer systems. If more waste water rushes into a treatment plant than can be handled, the overload causes raw sewage to wash into waterways and onto beaches, to back up into basements, or to leak from pipes.

Yet, unless the sewage disposal system fails to function in some way, there is seldom widespread public interest in what happens to waste water after it is carried away. But the proper treatment of waste water often determines whether or not people in a community will have clean waterways and water that is safe for drinking and agricultural use.

WASTE WATER DISPOSAL

Long before cities built sewer systems, waste water simply went back into the same rivers or lakes it came from. It was part of the natural cycle, maintaining adequate stream flow and balancing the ecological system that supported fish and wildlife (see *ecology*, in Glossary). In most cases, solid materials settled to the bottom of waterways, and as water moved downstream, bacteria and other microorganisms decomposed human waste and dead plant and animal matter.

If a river or lake is not overloaded with waste materials, the natural cleansing process still goes on. During decomposition, microorganisms make use of dissolved oxygen in the water. One measurement for water quality is the biological oxygen demand (BOD)—the amount of oxygen needed for biological decomposition of wastes. If the organic matter demands more oxygen than is available, water quality suffers.

As populations have grown and the amount of waste has increased, the BOD in waterways frequently has been grossly out of balance. Until about the mid-1900s, raw and treated sewage was routinely released into waterways and many rivers and streams in effect became extensions of sewer systems. The Delaware River, for example, was so polluted with sewage in the early 1940s that water in the Philadelphia harbor contained no oxygen, and the stinking mixture ate the paint off ships.

Even though sewage treatment today for the most part prevents the kind of putrid conditions suffered by the Delaware, waste water discharges still cause problems such as eutrophication (described earlier). In addition, to repeat what has become a major public health and environmental issue: many heavy metals and other toxic industrial chemicals that microorganisms cannot break down have increased in waste water.

According to the Environmental Protection Agency, most municipal waste treatment plants, which are equipped to treat human waste and other organic matter, are unable to remove large quantities of industrial chemicals. A federal program initiated in the 1970s requires that manufacturers pretreat waste water to reduce toxins before releasing the water into a municipal sewer system. But industries often resist spending the large sums required for pretreatment of waste water, and local governments have little authority to deal with businesses that do not comply with EPA standards. Public protests and political pressure are needed in some cases to bring about the pretreatment of industrial wastes.

TREATING WASTE WATER

What happens to waste water once it enters the disposal system? Pipelines and pumps transport it to a treatment plant for cleaning. At the plant, the cleansing process usually involves two major stages—primary and secondary treatment. In primary treatment, the sewage may be ground up and screened to remove large solid items such as sticks and toys. Smaller particles settle out in a sedimentation tank.

Primary treatment usually includes *flotation* and *coagulation*. Waste water in flotation tanks is saturated with air, and solid particles float to the surface to be skimmed off. Impurities in the water also may be collected by adding coagulants, substances such as alum, which bind particles together and form a fluffy mass known as floc. The floc can then be separated from the water in the sedimentation process.

The sediment, called *sludge*, is removed from the water and treated so that it can be hauled away and disposed of on land or at sea. In some cases, sludge is placed in airtight tanks where *anaerobic* bacteria (those that do not require oxygen) digest it, producing methane gas, which can be used as a fuel. The leftover sludge may be used as fertilizer.

In the secondary treatment stage, waste water separated from sludge is aerated—mixed with air in order to pump oxygen into it. Sometimes this is done by letting the water spray out of nozzles or running it over coke (a by-product of coal). Then the waste water is sprayed onto gravel beds where *aerobic* bacteria (those that do require oxygen) decompose

An estuary, where a river meets the sea
and fresh water and seawater mix, may be
a refuge for seabirds and other aquatic life.
This estuary is formed by the Santa Clara
River, which flows into the Pacific Ocean
between Ventura and Oxnard, California.
The area is part of a national park.

harmful materials. The water may then be released into a river, *estuary*, or sea.

Some treatment plants use a third stage, called tertiary treatment. Basically, the sedimentation and coagulation processes are repeated, and the water is filtered and disinfected. Other more complex processes may be used to remove such pollutants as mercury, phosphates, nitrates, and cyanide.

RECLAIMING AND RECYCLING WATER

Because of shortages of potable water in some parts of the United States, an increasing number of communities are reusing or recycling waste water that has received tertiary treatment, or whatever type of treatment is needed to safely reuse water for specific purposes. The state of California long has advocated water reclamation for irrigation, as was common practice for thousands of years in many parts of the world. Ancient Greek, Roman, and Asian societies, for example, used waste water for irrigation. So did Europeans during the sixteenth and seventeenth centuries. Today, advanced sewage disposal systems in some nations—Sweden and Switzerland, in particular—include treatment of sewage so that it can be put back on the land as fertilizer.

In California, only primary treatment may be needed to reuse waste water for irrigating orchards, vineyards, and seed crops. Tertiary treatment is required for irrigating food crops and parks and playgrounds. In some individual cases, waste water that has received tertiary treatment can be used to recharge groundwater. But because of possible health risks due to industrial pollutants in waste water, California regulations are very strict in regard to any human contact with reclaimed water.

[42]

Another problem in the reuse of waste water is public aversion—people find the idea of reclaimed water repulsive, even though the water could be quite safe for household purposes. But the same attitude does not seem to apply when cities discharge waste water that has received only secondary treatment into rivers; that same water usually is withdrawn downstream as a drinking water source.

The negative view of reclaiming waste water no doubt has slowed efforts in the United States to adopt dual (two) water systems, which are common in some European countries. In dual water supply systems, drinking water is piped to one or a few faucets in the home, and other pipes carry reclaimed (treated) water to use for flushing toilets, watering lawns, washing clothes, and other household purposes.

Some individual homeowners in California and other sections of the United States are beginning to make use of dual plumbing systems. And water districts and health departments in southern California are working with developers to construct high-rise buildings with dual systems. Reclaimed water, dyed blue for identification, would be piped into buildings for toilets and urinals. A few industries in California also are using treated municipal waste water for cooling and manufacturing processes. In-plant recycling of water is another method of reuse that helps reduce the amount of waste water (and toxic chemicals) discharged into sewer systems.

OTHER RECLAMATION PROJECTS

Another pioneering water reclamation project is under way in San Diego. The city is treating waste water in ponds filled with rapidly growing water hyacinth plants. Although the idea seems exotic, the

[43]

National Aeronautics and Space Administration (NASA) for some time has been conducting experiments with hyacinths, which thrive in raw sewage, to decompose organic matter and provide oxygen in space stations. Bacteria in the roots of hyacinths break down organic material so that it can be absorbed by the plants.

The San Diego process is less expensive than the secondary treatment method of aerating and heating sewage to maintain the proper balance of bacteria for decomposition. Water from the hyacinth ponds is used for irrigation purposes and helps San Diego in its overall efforts to increase reclaimed water use to 12 percent of total demand by the year 2010.

In other states, such as Georgia and Florida, waste water also is being returned to the land, helping to nourish woodlands, greenbelts near or in cities, golf courses, and parks. Treated waste water can be safely applied to the land when toxic contaminants have been removed. Plants, sun, and air can help cleanse water as can soils that serve as natural filters, allowing purified water to percolate into streams and eventually aquifers. This process has been called the circular system of water use, as opposed to the lineal system of water intake and then discharge of wastes out and far away.

Water expert John Sheaffer of Chicago has been advocating the idea of a circular system for many years. Sheaffer's engineering firm has designed a number of such treatment systems across the United States. One serves highly industrialized Muskegon, Michigan, and surrounding towns. Along with organic compounds that had to be controlled, chemical processing companies discharged a number of hazardous pollutants into the Muskegon system.

But the system, as verified by environmental research laboratories, has been able to remove contaminants from the waste water.

How does the circular system work? Basically the sewage is piped to storage lagoons, where floating churns help bacteria and oxygen begin the cleansing process, at the same time retaining nitrogen, phosphorus, and potassium for fertilizers. After treatment, the nutrient-rich water is sprayed onto crops such as field corn. Then, as water percolates through the soil and natural filters, it is collected in an underground network of drainpipes, and clean water eventually flows into streams for continued reuse.[20]

Although similar systems have succeeded in other parts of the United States and other regions of the world, they probably will not be widely adopted in the United States until widespread negative attitudes about waste water change. Also, officials in industries and government have vested interests in conventional waste water treatment and frequently oppose changes to traditional disposal plants. But the high costs of larger or improved sewage treatment plants may finally bring about alternative methods of waste water disposal. Some water experts believe that land application of waste water is vital to continued growth in arid regions. Other alternatives, such as basins to collect urban and agricultural runoff, also are needed to prevent the kinds of overflows that contaminate beaches or cause eutrophication of lakes and estuaries.

CHAPTER FOUR
VITAL LINKS— WETLANDS

Call it a swamp, slew, marsh, mire, bog, bottom-land, pond, or a wet meadow. These terms, and many others, are synonyms for wetlands, and frequently they are turned into verbs to express negative ideas: "bogged down in detail," "mired in misery," "swamped with work." Such expressions reflect the once common belief that wetlands were wastelands, of very little value except as places to dump trash and sometimes even to dispose of human bodies. Swamps or marshy areas have often been depicted as frightening, evil places, or at best unpleasant areas infested with mosquitoes, snakes, and other pests or vermin.

With such attitudes, is it any wonder that for centuries people worldwide have been filling in or draining wetlands? At the time of Julius Caesar's rule, for example, wetlands along the English coast were being "reclaimed"—or used for other purposes. Since the colonial period, Americans have destroyed or damaged more than half of the estimated 215 million acres (87 million hectares) of wetlands that originally existed. The graph in Figure 3 illustrates the staggering losses of our wetlands. Because

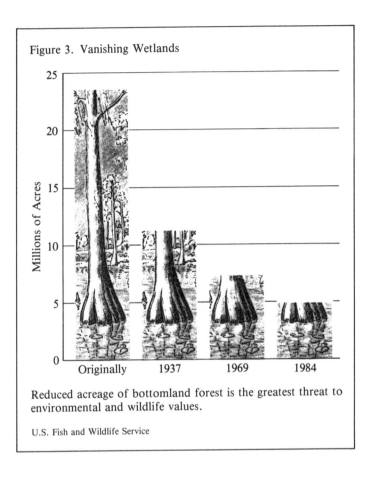

Figure 3. Vanishing Wetlands

Millions of Acres

Originally   1937   1969   1984

Reduced acreage of bottomland forest is the greatest threat to environmental and wildlife values.

U.S. Fish and Wildlife Service

people believed that wetlands were useless, these low-lying lands were filled in to build cities or were drained for farming. Many of the wetlands have been stripped of trees, mined for peat, phosphate, and other resources, or flooded for reservoirs. Often they are polluted with toxic wastes, sewage, or excess salt. During recent years, however, environmental groups and government agencies in the United States have been calling attention to the benefits of wetlands and the need to protect them.

[47]

WHERE ARE WETLANDS?

Before any widespread efforts could be made to save U.S. wetlands, the areas had to be identified and categorized. In general, wetlands can be defined as land where the water table is close to the surface or land that is covered with water for part of the growing season and supports plant life that can adapt to saturated soil or watery conditions. As the Environmental Protection Agency has pointed out, "A wide variety of wetlands have formed across the country due to regional and local differences in vegetation, hydrology, water chemistry, soils, topography, climate and other factors."[21]

The U.S. Fish and Wildlife Service began an analysis of the nation's wetlands during the 1970s, and set up a data base that would help regulatory agencies and private citizens make decisions about the wise use of wetlands. Although the classification system is somewhat specialized, most wetlands can be categorized as either coastal (seawater) or inland (freshwater).

Some wetlands are large, complex ecological systems, such as the Everglades in Florida, the Pocosins (an Algonquin term for "swamp on a hill") in the Southeast—particularly North Carolina—and the Nebraska Rainwater Basin. Other wetlands may form around small spring-fed ponds or along streams.

Coastal wetlands include those along the shores of the Atlantic and Pacific oceans and Gulf coasts. California's salt marsh along the San Francisco Bay is an example. Like most of the coastal wetlands in California, it is linked to an estuary, a bay or mouth of a river, where fresh water meets the sea. Plants and animals that live in estuarine marshes have been able to adapt to the varying levels of salt and low levels of dissolved oxygen in the waterlogged soils.

The names given to some types of inland wetlands suggest their characteristics: shrub bogs in northern states, wet tundras in Alaska, tropical rain forests in Hawaii. Riparian marshes, those along rivers and streams, are common types of inland wetlands where grasses, cattails, and bullrushes grow. Lake marshes, another type of wetland, also contain a variety of vegetation, including water lilies and underwater plants. Other wetlands are wooded swamps, known as bottomland hardwood forests, that form in southern states along flood plains or river valleys, particularly the Mississippi River.

In the Great Plains region and parts of the south-central Canadian provinces there are low areas on the prairie known as prairie potholes. Ranging in size from less than an acre to several square miles, these potholes periodically flood and dry out, depending on the seasons and weather conditions. Since prairie potholes are breeding grounds for more than half of North America's waterfowl, they also are called the "duck factories" of the continent.

Some wetlands are peat bogs, areas where the remains of mosses and other organic materials have accumulated over centuries. Dried peat is used for fuel in many European nations, and peat has been a source of energy on a limited basis in the United States.

WHY SAVE A SWAMP
(OR OTHER WETLAND)?

Although trappers and hunters have long appreciated the wildlife found in wetlands, only recently has the general public become aware of the benefits of these habitats. Many types of wildlife, including black bear, deer, waterfowl, and a large number of songbirds find food and refuge in wetlands. Marshes and swamps are home for such fur-bearing animals as mink, otter, beaver, nutria (a water-inhabiting rodent similar to the beaver),and muskrat. Each year the harvest of wildlife from U.S. wetlands is valued at several hundred million dollars. The total annual value of muskrat pelts alone is an estimated $70 million.

In the fall, ducks and geese migrate from northern wetlands to winter habitats in coastal wetlands of the Southeast and Southwest. Coastal wetlands also are spawning sites and nurseries for many types of fish and crustaceans (shellfish) such as shrimp and crab.

A variety of fish and shellfish feed on the plant and animal remains that have collected in the water. Thus destruction of wetlands affects offshore catches in such areas as the Gulf of Mexico. Fishing on the Great Lakes also has declined because of wetland losses. As the Council on Environmental Quality pointed out in its seventeenth annual report to Congress:

> Commercial and game fishes in the Great Lakes are dependent upon freshwater inland wetlands along the shore for spawning, feeding and shelter; declines in these stocks have been traced to the destruction of wetlands within the Great Lakes Basin. . . . Nearly all freshwater recreational fishing—a multibillion-dollar industry— is dependent upon wetlands.[22]

The timber from bottomland forests is another valuable resource from wetlands. White cedar trees in eastern swamps have provided shingles and posts.

In Alaska, wetlands produce fir and spruce trees, and from the South come oak, gum, and cypress— all have value as lumber or for manufacturing wood products.

Forested bottomlands, along with swamps, marshes, potholes, and other types of wetlands, are closely linked with the quality of the nation's water supply. Wetlands act as filters, taking in waste products from surface runoffs before water from the land reaches a lake, stream, river, or estuary. Some wetland plants can absorb toxic compounds, preventing them from reaching waterways or aquifers. However, if birds, fish, and animals eat the plants, there is some danger that poisonous substances can be passed up the food chain. Wetlands also filter out excess nitrogen and phosphorous that could create eutrophication in open waters. Estuarine wetlands along the Chesapeake Bay have in fact absorbed such a large amount of nutrients and toxic compounds since the 1950s that various fish and plants have been destroyed. Nevertheless, in most cases wetlands effectively protect water resources.

Another protective function is flood control. Wetlands can stem the overflow from streams, rivers, lakes, and other bodies of water. Trees, shrubs, vines, and other plants help store the overflow and prevent the water from moving rapidly into farmlands, residential areas, or urban centers. Slowing down the flow of flood waters limits soil erosion and damage to crops and buildings.

Many wetlands recharge aquifers, which provide fresh water for human use. The Florida Everglades is a prime example. Although much of the original Everglades has been converted to agriculture, huge areas have been set aside for water conservation. The marshes and swamps recharge the Biscayne

Aquifer, a source of potable water for more than 3 million people. Recharging from the Everglades also prevents intrusion of salt water into coastal aquifers.

Finally, millions of people value wetlands for their natural beauty and various recreational and educational opportunities. Nature walks, boating, sport fishing, bird-watching, wildlife studies, and nature photography are just a few of the leisure activities people enjoy in wetlands.

CAUSES OF WETLAND LOSSES

Even though there is more widespread understanding of the importance of preserving the ecology of wetlands, that cannot undo changes that have been made in many areas of the United States. More than half of the original wetlands have been converted to other uses. "These losses are continuing today at an alarming rate; an estimated 350,000 to 500,000 acres [about 141,600 to 202,300 hectares] annually," the Environmental Protection Agency noted in its report on water quality sent to Congress late in 1987.

How and why are wetlands being lost? Most losses have come about because wetlands have been drained and converted to agricultural or industrial use. In North Dakota nearly 50 percent of the state's original wetlands have been drained for farming. Kentucky also has lost half of its wetlands, and the EPA reports, "Nearly all of the areas that remain have been degraded by either pesticides, acid mine drainage, siltation, brine water, or domestic and industrial sewage."[23]

In southern states, an estimated 24 million acres (9.7 million hectares) of bottomland forests have dwindled to 5 million acres (2 million hectares).

Most of the acreage has been converted to agriculture. The forests are part of a large water-land system and link rivers, streams, coastal plains, and bays. Part of the year, the land floods with overflow from rivers and streams, depositing nutrients. When the waters recede, enriched soils remain, providing fertile land for crops.

Bottomland forests were first cleared to produce cotton, although that has not been the primary use of the land. More often bottomlands, especially in the lower Mississippi Valley, have been planted in soybeans, which grow rapidly and are a major cash crop.

As farmers were able to increase their incomes from soybeans, the methods for clearing and draining land improved. At the same time, the federal government increased support for flood control in bottomland areas. These factors and others have contributed to environmental damages in forested wetlands and also in surrounding areas. When there are drier conditions, fewer trees, shrubs, and plants grow to support and protect wildlife and fish, and their numbers decreased. With less vegetation, water flows more rapidly through the area and carries off soil and nutrients that may be deposited in lakes or estuaries, possibly leading to eutrophication. There is also runoff of pesticides and fertilizers from wetlands converted to agricultural use.

Urban development and state and local public-works projects are other contributing factors in the loss and damage of wetlands. Bridge and highway construction, dredging and clearing to install utility poles or to lay pipelines, logging, waste disposal in impoundment sites, and filling for railroad beds are among the many human activities that destroy coastal and inland marshes. Only half of Connecticut's original coastal marshes remain, for example. The wetlands along the Chesapeake Bay, the largest U.S. estuary, have been deteriorating for the past three decades due in part to pollutants from industry and sewage treatment plants. On the West Coast, urban sprawl has destroyed an estimated 75 percent of southern California's coastal wetlands from Santa Barbara to the border of Mexico.

Some natural events—droughts, erosion, rise in sea level, storms—also threaten wetlands. And in some areas, such as Louisiana's Gulf Coast, natural and human-induced factors combine to destroy wetlands. For example, Louisiana's coastal marshes first developed when deposits from the Mississippi River formed deltas along the coast. But as more and more people settled along the Gulf of Mexico, their activities affected the land and waterways. Levees were built to control flooding, and canals were dug for shipping and transportation. As a result, the river flow changed, sending deposits far out to sea. Rising Gulf waters have covered the marshes and salt water has intruded into surface waters.

CONSERVATION AND MANAGEMENT

To save some of the Louisiana wetlands, hydrologists and water management experts have suggested a number of protective measures. These include controlling further urban development in marsh areas, managing the river flow to increase silt deposits, and banning construction of new canals and plugging old ones. Yet some of these measures would be expensive and certainly would be controversial. At this time, few changes are expected in the near future, and wetland losses will probably be a matter of concern in the region for years to come.

Grasses, cattails, and a variety of other plants grow in marshes—wetlands—near Lake Michigan. Many of these wetlands have been preserved as part of state or national parks. Wetlands are homes for wildlife, including waterfowl and a large number of songbirds.

Not all threatened wetlands require such complex solutions to save them. However, it is never a simple matter of just saying no to hold off conversion to agricultural use or urban intrusion. In the first place, most wetlands are privately owned, primarily by farmers, ranchers, and corporations. Commercial and residential builders also own a good share of America's wetlands.

Landowners might realize the various ecological benefits and appreciate the natural beauty of a wetland area, but these values can be overshadowed by economic factors. A marsh, swamp, or bog might be home for wildlife that destroy cash crops, so a farmer may decide to drain the land. Or a farmer might decide to use wetlands to grow profitable foods or fiber. Developers may want to fill in wetlands in order to construct homes or businesses, which will of course be sold for a profit.

Nevertheless, some landowners have preserved wetlands by leasing them for hunting and trapping. Some have used their wetlands to grow hay or wild rice. Others have carefully managed timber harvests to preserve the ecology of their forested bottomlands.

Private groups and citizens who do not own wetlands have initiated a number of conservation efforts also. In New York City, for example, a group of residents in a housing complex were able to save a nearby wetland, the Thomas Pell Wildlife Sanctuary. The city administration wanted to turn the sanctuary into a landfill, but people in the housing complex organized strong protests and the city eventually dropped the plan.[24]

Thousands of Americans support private conservation groups with special programs to preserve wetlands. One of the oldest is the Izaak Walton League of America (IWLA), which began in the 1920s because sportspeople were concerned about declining water quality. Today, one of IWLA's programs, Wetland Watch, encourages people to adopt and protect local fresh water wetlands.

Another private organization, the Nature Conservancy, works to save endangered species and their habitats. Its volunteer members and paid staff also manage more than 1,000 nature preserves in the United States, including Virginia's Great Dismal Swamp.

Ducks Unlimited has been preserving and restoring wetlands in Canada, the United States, and Mexico since 1937. Because of droughts during the 1930s, the number of waterfowl dropped considerably. Concerned hunters organized to preserve habitats for ducks and geese. Ducks Unlimited now raises money for game preserves and for educational programs about the value of wetlands.

Although federal and state policies for the past few decades have encouraged the destruction of wetlands, government agencies have set up a variety of protective programs in recent years. Florida is one state that purchased millions of acres of wetlands and dredged canals or drained them for real estate development and rail lines. But there were many undesirable consequences, such as the lowering of the water table, which has caused land to sink and soil and vegetation to dry out. Drying conditions also caused fire hazards. Then in 1984, state legislators passed a Wetlands Protection Act and other regulations designed to control dredging, conserve fish and wildlife, protect endangered species, and improve water quality.

In Michigan where nearly 75 percent of the 11.2 million acres (4.5 million hectares) of wetlands have vanished, state laws now regulate wetlands and establish penalties for those who illegally alter these habitats. Most states have passed similar laws, which correspond to a major federal program, set up under Section 404 of the Clean Water Act. The 404 program, as it is called, requires that anyone who wishes to dredge, fill, or discharge material into U.S. waters, including most wetlands, must meet certain terms as spelled out in a permit from the Army Corps of Engineers.[25]

Other federal regulations that protect wetlands are part of the Food Security Act of 1985 and are known as the "Swampbuster" provisions. The regulations restrict or ban federal commodity payments and loans to farmers who produce crops on wetlands converted to farmland after the law was enacted. According to the U.S. Department of Agriculture, such provisions discourage conversion of wetlands to agricultural uses.[26]

Recent federal legislation also denies special tax credits or deductions, as were once allowed, to those who sell converted wetlands. Another law prohibits the use of federal funds for new construction in endangered habitats and also bans disaster insurance to rebuild in coastal wetland areas that are frequently damaged by storms.

A long-standing wetlands preservation program is the acquisition of wetlands. The federal government has purchased more than 3.6 million acres (about 1.5 million hectares) for wildlife refuges. Funds for these purchases come from hunting fees. Hunters must buy not only licenses but also stamps, called Duck Stamps, before they can hunt waterfowl. A number of states have set up "habitat stamp" programs also, using the funds for wildlife preservation and the purchase of wetlands.

Anyone who wants to get involved with programs to preserve wetlands can get information and sometimes technical assistance from such federal agencies as the Environmental Protection Agency, the Fish and Wildlife Service, and the Soil Conservation Service. State natural resource departments and county extension offices also can provide advice. Besides the private groups already mentioned, hunting clubs and state and local chapters of such organizations as the National Wildlife Federation and the National Audubon Society usually have information on how individuals and groups can help protect, conserve, or acquire wetlands.

CHAPTER FIVE
SCUM GREEN AND
ICE BLUE LAKES

WARNING
HIGH POLLUTION READINGS
ARE OFTEN FOUND IN
THESE WATERS

Bathe at your own risk.

It's a familiar sign, the type that has been posted frequently on the beaches and shores of many U.S. lakes. Some lakes are polluted with pathogens or toxic chemicals; others may be eutrophic, over-loaded with aquatic plants.

Thousands of lakes across the United States—more than 10,000 in twenty-three states reporting to the Environmental Protection Agency—are so over-nourished that algae and other primitive plant life grow rapidly, then decay, using up oxygen and lit-erally smothering the fish. Many more lakes, es-pecially in the Northeast, are acidified and so con-taminated with heavy metals that they are unable to support aquatic life.

SMALL LAKES, BIG PROBLEMS

It's called Clear Lake. But this small, shallow lake in LaPorte, a city on the fringe of the heavily industrialized area of northern Indiana, is hardly clear. In fact, the lake is so full of weeds, the city's Park and Recreation Department was ready to launch a weed-killing project during the summer of 1989. A number of fund-raisers had been held the previous year to help pay for cleanup of the lake, and citizens were beginning to grumble about lack of action.

However, Gary Doxtater, a biologist with the state's Department of Natural Resources, advised that LaPorte carefully plan its lake cleanup. "Killing the weeds and letting them sink to the bottom of the lake would provide nutrients for even more weeds to grow," Doxtater explained. He added that because the lake is shallow, sunlight reaches the bottom, helping the weeds to grow quickly.

Excess nutrients probably have come into the lake from farms, septic systems, golf courses, streets, and parking lots. But runoff from a golf course is quite different from farm or street runoff. A study of the lake's *watershed*, which consists of all water flowing into the lake, would show the sources of runoff and help determine what action should be taken, Doxtater said. One of the first steps would likely be construction of a basin that would catch *sediments*— soil and other particles—before they reach the lake.

The problems of Clear Lake are similar to what has happened to Shipshewana Lake, in a predominantly rural area of northern Indiana. One observer noted that the lake "is as green as the grass." But another said the lake's color was more like "scum green."

[61]

Shipshewana Lake is loaded with algae and other aquatic plants, which has led to fish kills. Water quality officials have declared the 200-acre (80-hectare) body of water "dead." Marshes once surrounded the lake and filtered runoff from farm fields, animal feeding lots, septic systems, and roads. But as with many other U.S. wetlands, the marshes were destroyed to build homes.

"I can understand people wanting to live next to a lake," one water official said. "It's a dream place for many people, but that dream dies when the lake dies. People have to understand that a lake has to be a lake, and it has its own ecology, which should be protected. Otherwise there will be huge expenses to clean up and save the lake."

Huge expenses are exactly what many state and local government agencies across the United States have experienced as they have undertaken lake restoration projects. South Dakota and Minnesota, for example, spent at least $850,000, along with the same amount provided by the EPA, just to begin cleanup of Big Stone Lake, which borders both states. According to the EPA:

> Big Stone Lake is hypereutrophic and receives high loads of nutrients from its tributaries. Lengthy algae blooms and excessive weed growth have been observed in the lake. As a

Fishing and taking a dip in the "ol' swimming hole" are just two activities that many people can enjoy—if waterways are kept clean.

[63]

result, recreational usage and property values have declined. Erosion from cropland and run-off from livestock operations have been identified as major sources of pollution. Other sources include municipal discharges, food processing wastes, streambank and lakeshore erosion, and erosion from construction activities.[27]

How can these multiple problems be solved? As part of the plan to reduce nutrient and sediment overloads in the lake, the EPA, the U.S. Department of Agriculture, and state agricultural and conservation officials have urged operators of animal feedlots, which contribute the largest amount of pollutants to the lake, to construct waste management systems. Such a system may include biological treatment of animal wastes to reduce the nutrient content. Or the system might involve storing manure in concrete bins and then carefully applying manure on fields so that plants make maximum use of the fertilizer and runoff of nutrients is reduced.

The lake restoration plan also calls for farmers to use "best management practices," which generally are the most effective practical means of preventing or reducing pollution. These may include conserving irrigation water, controlling soil erosion, and limiting use of *agrochemicals*.

Recovering wetlands, controlling waste water disposal, and preventing erosion of streambanks and riverbanks are other measures being taken to restore Stone Lake and hundreds of smaller lakes in Minnesota. Nearly 8,000 lakes in the state have been classified as having high nutrient levels.

Eutrophication is a "significant problem," as the EPA put it, in about half the states, "particularly in areas where smaller lakes are subjected to persistent urban, recreational, and agricultural pressures."[28]

[64]

SAVE OUR LAKE
REVISITED

The Great Lakes also are under pressure from human activities that have deteriorated water quality. Lakes Superior, Michigan, Huron, Erie, and Ontario provide drinking water, recreational opportunities, and transportation for millions of people in the United States and Canada. About one-seventh of the total U.S. population and one-third of the Canadian population live within the Great Lakes basin, an area that includes parts of New York, Pennsylvania, Ohio, Indiana, Illinois, Wisconsin, Minnesota, and most of Michigan, plus parts of the provinces of Ontario and Quebec.

Although there have been some improvements in the Great Lakes since the 1960s, there are still many trouble spots. Fish populations have increased in Lake Erie, for example, but the warm temperature and relatively shallow waters of the lake make it a prime environment for nutrient overload. In addition, Ohio harbor areas on Lake Erie are still polluted with metals from industries, urban runoff, overflows from sewers, seepage from septic tanks, and contaminated sediments.

Toxic contamination of sediments is a "common problem in Great Lakes harbors and bays which, in turn, can affect aquatic life and serve as a continuing source of toxins to the larger lake system," the EPA noted in its 1986 report to Congress.[29] The report also concluded that toxic substances such as mercury, polychlorinated biphenyls (PCBs)—synthetic compounds that were once used in industry but are now banned—and pesticides such as DDT (also banned) continue to contaminate fish. The toxic compounds do not break down and may be stored in the fatty tissue of fish and also in people

[65]

who eat the fish. As a result, fishing is restricted or prohibited in some areas of the Great Lakes.

Toxic chemicals also harm Great Lakes water birds, say ecologists who have been studying water-fowl species that nest in northern regions, such as Michigan's Saginaw Bay area and on an island in Lake Superior. Researchers have found high concentration of PCBs, which they believe have been blown into the lakes from hundreds of miles away. In a 1986–88 survey, the ecologists saw a 31 percent increase in deformities among newly hatched birds compared to those found in the 1960s and 1970s. Many birds were born with eye defects, club feet, crossed beaks, malformed hips, and body organs attached outside their bodies.

Hundreds of chemical contaminants enter the Great Lakes by seeping from industrial waste sites or landfills. Discharges from sewage disposal systems or emissions from industrial plants may pollute the waters. At times, the death of fish and plants provides evidence of contaminants. Other times, toxic pollutants in lake waters cannot be seen and barely can be measured. But even trace amounts of some chemicals can be hazardous to aquatic life and to human health.

One of the major difficulties with many human-produced compounds is that they bioaccumulate, or build up in the food chain. For example, microscopic plants and animals called *plankton* may absorb toxins in the water; small fish eat the plankton, and poisonous dose after dose builds up. Larger fish feed on small fish and accumulate even greater quantities of toxic chemicals.

The accumulative effect of Mirex, another pesticide that is now banned, has been documented in the Niagara River and Lake Ontario. Although the amounts of Mirex were minute, fish in Lake Ontario had accumulated several hundred times the amount that would be acceptable for human consumption, leading to a total ban on fishing for several years. Some fishing is allowed now, but several species of fish are contaminated with PCBs, Mirex, and dioxin.

The term "dioxin" actually refers to a group of highly toxic chemicals that are unwanted by-products of some manufacturing processes or of waste-burning operations. Dioxins include seventy-five different chemical compounds, the most toxic being 2,3,7,8 tetrachlorodibenzo-p-dioxin (TCDD), a by-product in the manufacture of herbicides. Very small amounts of dioxin can cause a wide range of health problems, including severe headaches, sleeplessness, skin disorders, birth defects, and suppression of the body's immune system, which leaves a person susceptible to diseases.

Other problem areas on the Great Lakes include the Indiana Harbor Ship Canal, formed by two branches of the Calumet River. The canal empties into the southern end of Lake Michigan and carries a variety of toxic materials as it drains a heavily populated and highly industrialized area. High levels of pesticides and PCBs have been found in fish from the southern part of the lake, although there has been a total decline in such contaminants since the 1970s.

A vast array of obstacles must be overcome to clean up the Great Lakes, many of which are covered in William Ashworth's book *The Late, Great Lakes*. Not the least of the difficulties is what to do about the contaminated sediments in the lakes. As sludge accumulates in harbors, waters become more and more shallow. Harbors are then dredged, and

Sludge tractors undertake the expensive task of removing sediment from Lake Barcroft, Virginia.

the sludge is loaded onto barges and towed off to deeper waters of a lake, where it is dumped. But once dumped, no one knows what happens to the chemical muck. Ashworth asked the unanswerable question: "What sort of Frankenstein's Monster are we building down there, deep in the once-beneficial sediments beneath the beds of the greatest reservoirs of fresh water on the face of the earth?"[30]

Another major problem is how to prevent the lakes from being dumping grounds for toxic materials in the first place. With so many nonpoint sources of pollution and so many different toxic compounds and so little knowledge about their effects, solutions are not going to come easily. There will be no "quick fixes." Ashworth believes too that public apathy makes the situation even worse. Many (if not most) of the Canadians and Americans who depend on the Great Lakes for drinking water and other purposes are not even aware of polluted water in their backyards. Some people simply accept the fact that there are problems but feel they can do little about them.

Yet there are some efforts under way—again—to "save" the Great Lakes. A number of private citizens' groups have been formed to work for legislation or take other actions that will preserve the water quality of the lakes. National environmental groups have set up committees to deal with Great Lakes problems. International, federal, and state agencies are monitoring the lakes for toxic contamination and are supporting research programs on how to reduce toxins.

Through international agreements, Canada and the United States are working together to control the discharge of phosphorus into the Great Lakes. Since the 1960s, phosphorus levels have been controlled and reduced in the upper lakes, but additional controls are needed for the lower lakes. Better management of agricultural runoff could relieve some of the overload, experts say.

In another joint effort, the United States and Canada are monitoring the St. Mary's, St. Clair, and Detroit rivers, and Lake St. Clair—channels that connect the Great Lakes. Research is under way to determine the effects of toxins in the channels. It has been learned that much of the pollution originates from a huge petrochemical complex in Ontario, Canada.

The states and provinces within the Great Lakes basin also are trying to protect the quantity as well as quality of their water supply. Over the years, various proposals have been made to divert water from the Great Lakes to meet the needs of drier regions, but the idea has created a great deal of heated debate. A committee representing each participating state and province was formed to work with the U.S. Geological Survey (USGS) to create a data base on regional water use. The information will help "predict the effects on lake levels of proposed withdrawals, diversions, and consumptive use," USGS reported.[31] By working together, the members hope to conserve and manage their water resources to benefit the entire region.

ICE BLUE ACIDIC LAKES

International and interstate agreements, plus federal controls, may help solve another lake pollution problem: acidity. Surface waters become acidic when runoffs from mine tailings (or wastes) and air pollutants enter the water. Air pollutants fall as what is popularly known as acid rain, which includes rain, snow, dew, fog, and dry particles.

Acidic compounds form in the atmosphere when oxides of sulfur and nitrogen react with water, sunlight, and oxygen. Usually, the sources of pollution are gases emitted when fossil fuels—particularly coal and oil—are burned. Sulfur dioxide emissions from power plants and oxides of nitrogen from motor vehicle exhausts are the main culprits, although other gases from industries may also form acidic compounds that are part of acid rain. Winds and clouds may transport the atmospheric pollutants for miles before they fall on land and water.

Acidity is measured on a pH (potential for hydrogen) scale, diagrammed in Figure 4. A pH of 7 is neutral; a pH below 7 indicates acid, above 7 is alkaline. The pH scale, which ranges from 0 to 14, is logarithmic, so each unit marks a tenfold change. Lemon juice, at pH2, is ten times more acidic than apple juice, at pH3, while baking soda (pH8) is ten times more alkaline than blood (a little above pH7).

Normal rainfall is not neutral since such natural events as volcanic eruptions, lightning, and forest fires produce acids. Usually rain measures about pH5.6 to pH5; precipitation that measures below is considered acidic. Along the eastern seaboard of the American continent, annual rainfall has registered about pH4 in some areas, sometimes dropping to 3.5, almost as acidic as lemon juice. In areas of western Europe, Scandinavia, and Japan, the pH values of precipitation have ranged from 3.5 to 5.5.

Not all water bodies become acidic because of acid rain. Soils in some parts of the United States, such as the Midwest, contain minerals (limestone for example) that can buffer or neutralize acids. But in

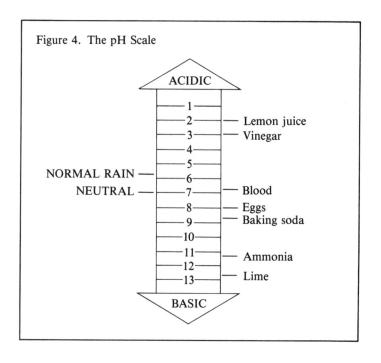

Figure 4. The pH Scale

ACIDIC

1
2 — Lemon juice
3 — Vinegar
4
5
NORMAL RAIN — 6
NEUTRAL — 7 — Blood
8 — Eggs
9 — Baking soda
10
11 — Ammonia
12
13 — Lime

BASIC

the northeastern part of the continent, many lakes are underlain with solid granite, which has little or no buffering capacity. Glacial soils also lack the minerals to neutralize acids in runoff before they reach lakes, ponds, or rivers.

What happens to a lake and its aquatic life when water becomes acidic? At pH5, frogs, salamanders, and shellfish die off and zooplankton, food for fish and other animals, disappear. Below pH5, most newly hatched fish die and those that survive may be malformed or dwarfed. Mature fish often die when there is a "pulse" or surge of acids, which frequently happens during a spring thaw. The concentration of acids is released in a snow melt, entering a lake in runoff and causing "acid shock."

Acidified lakes may appear pure—clean and ice blue. But usually that is a sign that little life remains in the water, not even bacteria to decompose the leaves and twigs that fall to the bottom. The number of "acid dead" lakes has increased steadily since the 1970s, when articles on the effects of acid rain began to appear in popular magazines and major news-papers. Recent reports indicate that 25 percent of the lakes and ponds in New York's vast Adirondack Park are so acidic that fish cannot survive. Massa-chusetts reported more than 200 acidified water-bodies that no longer can support animal and plant life.

In Ontario, Canada, more than 300 lakes are acidic, with thousands more categorized as "acid sensitive," meaning they could soon become too acidic for aquatic life. Other nations have reported even worse conditions: Of the 90,000 lakes in Swe-den, 20,000 have pH values below 5; 4,000 are "dead," being no longer able to support fish. Eighty percent of Norway's surface waters are too acidic to support aquatic life or will soon be that way.

Acid deposition has other effects on water quality. Acid rain may draw heavy metals from soils and sed-iments. Mercury has been found in surface waters worldwide. Scientists long have believed that mer-cury entered lakes and streams only from soil runoff or was released from bedrock. But recent studies have shown that mercury is also washed from the air into surface waters. "Direct deposit of mercury from the air, combined with the acidity, makes the mercury more accessible to the fish," Gary Glass, an EPA researcher in Minnesota, reported. He noted also that fish taken from lakes with the great-est acid deposition have higher mercury levels than fish taken from other midwestern lakes.[32]

CHAPTER SIX
TROUBLE IN
RIVER CITY

DEAD CATS, TOXINS AND TYPHOID is how *Time* magazine headlined an article describing the pollutants in New River, which cuts across the California-Mexico border. New River carries toxins such as PCBs and benzene from factories, and viruses, including polio, and bacteria from human and livestock wastes. Cleaning up the contaminated waters is the responsibility of both California and Mexico and costs for cleanup are expected to be in the hundreds of millions of dollars. [33]

The Mexican river may be one of the dirtiest on the continent, but a number of rivers worldwide are also in trouble. In addition, as urban populations have grown, so have the problems of protecting the quality of waterways. Consider these events of the past few years.

- Hundreds of thousands of fish and eels were killed when a chemical warehouse caught fire and water hoses washed 30 tons of agrochemicals into the Rhine River in West Germany. Even before the accident the Rhine was known as the dirtiest river in Europe. About one-fifth of the world's chemical companies are situated along the Rhine and release wastes into the river, which is also the source of drinking water for 20 million people.

- Beluga whales were found dying in the St. Lawrence River in Canada. The whales were said to be "riddled with toxic chemicals," which were believed to have been discharged into the river from a Canadian aluminum company. However, the company insisted there was no connection between its industrial activities and deaths of the whales.
- In the United States, a New York research group found that at least 182,000 pounds (81,900 kg) of lead from agricultural and urban runoff made its way into the Hudson River each year. The lead contaminated the waterway for 150 miles (241 km) between Manhattan and Troy, New York.
- Seven barges on the Ohio River struck pilings and spilled 40,000 gallons (151,400 liters) of gasoline. Although the river is not a source of drinking water for most communities along the river, Louisville, Kentucky, 100 miles (160.9 km) downstream, had to close its water system intakes until the gasoline flowed past.
- Louisiana's Department of Environmental Quality found that fish in the Calcasieu River system were laced with toxic chemicals and warned against eating them. The cause? Petrochemical industries in the surrounding Lake Charles area had been discharging wastes into the waterways for years.

WATER QUALITY—GOOD AND BAD NEWS

In spite of numerous stories about polluted rivers, the quality of water in rivers and streams, like the quality of other waterbodies, is determined by use.

Water from streams may be used for industrial cooling and would not have to be as high in quality as water used for swimming or fishing. However, most waterways have more than one use, and judging the water quality may require weighing many variables and possible pollutants at different points along a stream or river.

Scientists who conducted a long-term study of 300 major U.S. rivers reported in 1987 that water quality had improved somewhat between 1974 and 1981, with "widespread decreases in fecal bacteria and lead concentrations." Such changes, the researchers noted in a *Science* report, came about because of the $100 billion in improvements to municipal sewage treatment plants and restricted use of leaded gasoline.

However, along with the good news comes the bad: the researchers found higher levels of nitrates due to agricultural runoff and acid rain. Concentrations of cadmium and arsenic were also high. Arsenic, poisonous to humans, frequently is a component of pesticides. Cadmium compounds are extremely toxic at low levels and can cause heart disorders and high blood pressure. Only 0.05 ppm (parts per million) are allowed in drinking water. A portion of the higher cadmium and arsenic levels was traced to industrial discharges into rivers. But the researchers concluded that another source of these contaminants was air pollutants—emissions from coal-fired power plants and industries, especially in the Midwest.[34]

Another report for the U.S. Geological Survey noted that toxic metals and synthetic organic compounds are "potentially more hazardous" than some other types of wastes discharged into waterways. Metals such as mercury and lead have low solubility, and many synthetic compounds "adhere to or adsorb sediments" in rivers and streams. As a result, toxic materials such as PCBs can accumulate at the bottom of waterways and then be absorbed by plants or ingested by bottom-feeding fish.[35] Toxins also can stay buried in sediments for long periods. But if rivers are flooded or dredged, or sediments are stirred up by currents or fish at the bottom, the toxins can be resuspended into the water.

THE PCB CONNECTION

Citizens who live along the Pigeon River in Cocke County, Tennessee, are understandably upset about the putrid water that flows past their homes and businesses. During the summer of 1988 the river was described as "a sludgy mess that looks like oily coffee and smells as bad as rotten eggs."[36]

What has caused such pollution? Reportedly the problem stems from wastes generated by Champion International Corporation, a paper mill 50 miles (80 km) upstream in Canton, North Carolina. Ever since its founding in the early 1900s, the mill has discharged its waste water into the Pigeon, which conveniently and with little expense to the company carries the sludge away. As a result, the river in Canton is clear and clean, a favorite recreation and fishing waterway. For this reason and the fact that Champion is a major employer in Canton, few people speak out against the company's waste disposal practices.

However, downstream in Tennessee, people have long complained about the paper mill. But they have had little success in getting Champion to clean up. After a lawsuit brought by Cocke County, the company agreed to bleach its wastes. Yet bleaching the sludge has done little or nothing to protect people from any health threats posed by pollutants, and may be creating even worse contamination.

According to a recent report from Greenpeace, an international environmental organization, more than 150 pulp and paper mills in North America are dumping hundreds of different chlorinated compounds, among them dioxin, in nearby rivers. In the papermaking process, some pulp mills use chlorine gas to "cook" and bleach wood pulp. The chlorine gas then reacts with compounds in wood pulp to create toxic chlorinated compounds called organochlorines, which include dioxins. "An average-sized paper mill discharges between 35 and 50 tons of chlorinated compounds every day" into waterways or the atmosphere, the Greenpeace report noted.[37]

Dioxin has been found in fish caught in the Wisconsin River, downstream from several pulp mills. On the Fox River, which empties into Green Bay and then Lake Michigan in northern Wisconsin, fifteen pulp and paper mills discharge wastes into the waterways. Analyses of fish and waterbirds that feed on fish in the rivers have shown what appears to be harmful concentrations of dioxin.

A number of surveys over the past decade indicate that paper mills as well as other industries have made some progress in controlling discharges of toxins into waterways. But the problem is far from solved, and there are still many unknowns in regard to the effects of synthetic chemical compounds. This was pointed out by New York State's Department of Environmental Conservation (DEC), which also has been working to clean up PCBs, particularly in the Niagara River, a link between Lake Erie and Lake Ontario.

A report in a DEC publication, *The Conservationist*, explained that discharges of toxins into the Niagara River from industries and sewage treatment plants and nonpoint sources such as hazardous waste sites have decreased significantly. But some contaminants are "lodged in pockets of nearshore bottom sediments, where [they] have accumulated since . . . early in this century." New York State is cooperating with federal and Canadian officials in putting together data on conditions of the Niagara River and Lake Ontario. The task involves developing complex computer programs to show cause-and-effect relationships, but such models are still in the development stage. As the DEC report noted:

> Scientists are not yet certain what harm is done by existing levels of toxins or the present discharge of trace amounts. Little is known about the effect of a mixture of toxins on aquatic organisms or humans. There is dispute about what it means when a factor which we are measuring increases or decreases. Further, scientists have very limited ability to predict how aquatic systems will change if chemical or physical input changes. . . .[38]

Meantime, down by the fishing streams (and lakes) health departments in New York and in other states continue to post advisories on what types of fish and game should not be eaten or should be restricted in the diet. New York's DEC noted that "recommendations are based on evaluation of contaminant levels in fish and wildlife."

For example, the department advises people not to eat carp from the Buffalo River in Erie County and Irondequoit Bay or smallmouth bass from the

Salmon River's mouth to the Salmon Reservoir. The advice also applies to a number of species in the St. Lawrence River and Niagara River below the Niagara Falls and Lake Ontario.

Recommendations also have been made for other New York waters, and in general people are advised not to eat more than one meal per week of fish from any water in New York. The health department cautions further that women of childbearing age and children under fifteen should not eat any fish with elevated contaminant levels.

MORE SOURCES OF POLLUTION

Like acid lakes, acidic conditions in some rivers are caused by atmospheric deposition that comes from emissions of sulfur dioxide and oxides of nitrogen. Some rivers and streams in the United States, Canada, Europe, and Asia have become so acidified that trout, salmon, and other species of fish have diminished in number or disappeared altogether.

Mining activities are another source of acid compounds in waterways. Runoff from mine or mill tailings and seepage from mines transport heavy metals into streams and rivers across the United States. In the western part of Maryland and the surrounding Appalachian states, for example, "acid mine drainage is the most serious water pollution problem," according to Maryland's environmental and health departments. "The low pH values and high levels of heavy metals are lethal to aquatic life" in a number of creeks and streams, and the north branch of the Potomac River, the departments reported.[39]

Mining operations of course require digging into the earth, which causes erosion and sedimentation in rivers and streams. These factors can affect waterways miles downstream from active mines. To make matters worse, contaminants often come from abandoned mines and seldom are there public or private funds to restore the land.

Erosion also comes about because of logging and road building required to get to stands of timber. Such activities frequently take place in western national forests on lands that easily erode, washing sediment into creeks and streams. This in turn destroys habitats where salmon and trout spawn. As a result, millions of dollars' worth of fish have been destroyed.

Although improvements have been made in controlling sewage discharge into rivers, the water quality of some rivers is still very poor because of municipal and industrial *effluents*. An example is New Jersey's Cooper River, which the Environmental Protection Agency said is "highly degraded." At the upper part of the river, the quality of the water is fairly good but "rapidly worsens . . . as it flows through Camden and adjoining towns." The river receives not only excessive waste discharges, but also is contaminated with urban storm-water runoff and pesticides that have accumulated in sediments and been found in fish. A hazardous waste site is also located within this river basin.

CHANGING IN MIDSTREAM

The Kissimmee River in Florida used to meander around and about landforms and filter through marshes as rivers naturally are prone to do. It meandered for 98 miles (158 km) from lakes in central Florida through a basin into Lake Okeechobee. Now, the river is only half as long. During the 1940s, the U.S. Army Corps of Engineers, under the direction of a Florida flood control project, straightened the course of the Kissimmee, making it a wide channel and devastating many wetlands that once lined its banks. Along with a network of levees and canals, channelization of the Kissimmee River was designed to carry flood waters quickly out of the river basin and regulate water in Lake Okeechobee. South of the lake, canals were built to drain the Everglades for agricultural purposes.

The rush of water from the Kissimmee River and the lack of wetlands along its banks have contributed to pollution problems in Lake Okeechobee. The lake's water quality is degraded because of increased nutrients and pesticide runoffs. In addition, the Everglades have been threatened.

By the early 1970s, Florida had set up a water management district to protect its wetlands and water supplies. Part of the Kissimmee River course has been changed again, back to its natural channel, with the expectation that marshes will come back too, along with wildlife and fish. Still, there are many problems to overcome. Changes in the hydrology of the river basin have led to lower water tables and subsidence. Salt water intrudes into canals and aquifers, and soils have degraded also.

Diverting the flow of a waterway is at the heart of a heated debate about the Platte River. The headwaters of the north branch of the Platte are in Wyoming while the south branch stems from Colorado, with the two forks joining in Nebraska, eventually emptying into the Missouri River south of Omaha. Denver is proposing to build a dam on the South Platte to provide water for its growing population. Another dam has been proposed for the Casper, Wyoming, area on the North Platte.

But the Audubon Society, National Wildlife Federation, and other conservation groups have strongly opposed the dams. Conservationists point out that the dam in the Denver area would destroy the environment, particularly in habitat near Kearney, Nebraska, which is famous as a feeding ground and sanctuary for cranes. In the spring, these huge birds rest and find mates in the river's wetlands as they migrate from Mexico and Texas to Canada and Alaska.

Although destroying wetlands has often proved disastrous not only for wildlife but also for human populations, dam proponents believe that the daily water needs of people come first. Yet as a *Newsweek* report explained it: "Roughly half of Denver's water is consumed not by people but by lawns and golf courses."[40]

CHAPTER SEVEN

SEAS OF DEBRIS

Along the shores of New Jersey, people are used to seeing an occasional diseased or dying dolphin wash ashore. That is part of the natural order. But within a few weeks in July 1987, at least 750 and perhaps over 1,000 bottlenose dolphins—half of the Atlantic dolphin population—washed up on New Jersey's beaches. Some dolphins were gasping for breath before they died. Many of the carcasses were covered with sores.

Researchers with the National Oceanic and Atmospheric Administration (NOAA) launched an investigation that lasted for many months, finally issuing a report in February 1989. Wildlife specialist Joseph Geraci, who headed the NOAA research team, said the dolphins were poisoned after eating fish contaminated with brevertoxin, a poison found in the algae blooms known as red tides.

Other scientists immediately questioned the NOAA findings since no large scale deaths have occurred among dolphins in the Gulf of Mexico, where red tides are common. Also, NOAA's own study showed that the dolphins had taken in huge amounts of PCBs, DDT, and other toxic chemicals. One animal reportedly had 6,800 ppm of PCBs in

*Sea lions and other marine mammals are
often the victims of polluted coastal waters
off the United States and other
industrialized nations.*

its blubber. EPA's "safe" level of PCBs in fish is 2 ppm. As a Greenpeace worker put it: "Many of [the dolphins] were swimming Superfund sites."

Greenpeace has been highly critical of the study, charging that the researchers planned to ignore the possibility of chemical poisoning. Members of Congress also reviewed the findings and ended up with more questions than answers about the dolphin die-off.

DON'T GO NEAR THE WATER
—OR BEACH

Dead sea life has not been the only problem along the nation's seacoasts. Beach closings became a regular part of recent summers. Paper, cans, bottles, plastics, decomposed rats, and medical wastes such as used hypodermic needles and swabs cluttered New York and New Jersey beaches.

Investigations have failed to determine the sources of all medical wastes. But according to Kathryn O'Hara of the Center for Marine Conservation (CMC), "New research suggests that most plastic syringes found [on beaches] during the summer 1988 were actually insulin-type disposal units used by diabetics and often discarded in toilets or trash . . . there may be a direct correlation between sewage systems and medical debris."[41]

Some garbage and trash on coastlines wash in from ships that dump at sea. Beaches also are contaminated with spillage from barges carrying waste to landfills. Another contributing factor is the tremendous population increase along coastlines and the Gulf of Mexico. More than 70 percent of the U.S. population lives on or near seacoasts; more people means a heavier burden of pollution.

While garbage on beaches may be nauseating and present some dangers to human health, it is only one type of hazard to the coastal environment. In fact, a congressional committee declared early in 1989 that coastal waters are being threatened from many sources. "The signs of damage and loss are pervasive," a published report stated. Unfortunately, there are plenty of examples to support the committee's conclusion.

Boston Harbor is at the top of the list. Although Boston began moving ahead in the late 1980s to clean up its harbor and coastline, Boston's entrance to the sea has been called a cesspool. Pollution of the harbor has been caused by outmoded and ineffective sewage treatment plants that serve forty-three metropolitan communities. According to an EPA director for the region: "Each day those plants discharge approximately a half billion gallons of partly treated sewage and approximately 70 tons of sludge into the harbor. The plants are so limited that their capacity is exceeded every time a good rain falls; as a result, millions of gallons of untreated sewage . . . [are released] directly into the harbor."[42]

What happens to aquatic life in Boston Harbor? Winter flounder caught near one of the treatment plants have higher concentrations of PCBs and DDT than any fish tested along the East Coast. Shellfishing is banned in part of the harbor and those caught in other areas must go through a purification process. Harbor beaches are often closed to swimmers because of health hazards. It is hoped that agreements to end sludge dumping, new waste water treatment facilities, and discharge farther out in the Massachusetts Bay will bring some solutions to Boston Harbor.

Down the eastern seaboard, examples include

more bays and inlets, such as New York Harbor, with its chemical brew, and Long Island Sound, where divers have found everything from discarded lawn furniture to dying eels and lobsters smothering from lack of oxygen. Contaminated rivers that empty into the Sound and excessive algae growth brought about by acid rain and nutrients from raw sewage that flows into the Sound have caused massive kills of sea life.

A 1988 study by the Environmental Defense Fund (EDF) found that oxides of nitrogen, a component in acid rain, is contributing to eutrophic conditions—excessive algae blooms—all along the eastern seaboard, especially in Maryland's Chesapeake Bay. Although the bay has been the focus of a vast cleanup program by both public and private groups, the estuary still is threatened by low dissolved oxygen levels because of eutrophication. It is also contaminated with high concentrations of toxic compounds from nonpoint sources. As a result, fish eggs and *larvae* have been destroyed, contributing to millions of dollars in losses to commercial fisheries.

The story is the same in other coastal waterways. In North Carolina, "dead water" zones in the Albemarle and Pamlico sounds send crabs scrambling from the water in search of oxygen. Young tarpon have been disappearing along Florida's southern coast, which marine experts believe may be due to pesticides, particularly DDT, in sediments. Toxic chemicals and heavy metals contaminate Louisiana estuaries, parts of Galveston Bay and the Gulf of Mexico, some of California's bays, particularly San Francisco Bay, and Oregon's coastal waterways.

Areas of Puget Sound along Washington's coast are so contaminated that they are on EPA's Superfund list of hazardous waste sites. The Superfund list includes more than a thousand land and water sites that have been disposal areas for hazardous materials. In 1980, the Comprehensive Environmental Response, Compensation, and Liability Act (known as Superfund) was set up to help pay the cleanup costs. However, only forty-three of the designated sites have been contained or restored.[43]

TIES THAT BIND AND KILL

Plastic bags. Plastic net. Plastic fishing lines. Plastic packaging materials. Plastic six-pack rings. Plastic binding straps. Polymer plastic products number in the thousands, and manufacturers are continually finding new uses for this petrochemical material made from oil or natural gas. Although plastic was first produced more than 100 years ago, it was not widely manufactured until World War II, when metal was scarce. Because the material is versatile, lightweight, and yet strong, and often less costly to produce than metals, plastic has been called "a modern miracle." But plastic products have become a severe pollution problem. Most plastics are not degradable and can have life spans of hundreds of years, thus straining the capacity of landfills.

Plastic throwaways also litter beaches worldwide. On U.S. shores, just a few hours of cleanup work can yield thousands of plastic products. The Center for Marine Conservation, which was first established in 1972 as the Center for Environmental Education, cited these examples:

- Along an Oregon shore, a crew found nearly 49,000 chunks of Styrofoam.
- On a stretch of North Carolina beaches, volunteers picked up more than 8,000 plastic bags in a few hours.

[89]

- A cleanup crew working for just three hours picked up 15,600 six-pack rings along the Texas coastline.
- Along a short stretch of beach in New Jersey, a volunteer cleanup crew found 650 tampon applicators.[44]

When discarded on shores or in waterways, plastic products can become death traps for fish, waterfowl, and sea animals. An estimated 2 million seabirds and 100,000 sea mammals die each year because of plastic pollution.

How do plastics cause death? Many aquatic animals and birds are entangled in plastic fish nets or in packaging materials such as plastic hoops and net bags for vegetables and fruits. Entangled creatures may strangle, or may starve because they are unable to swim or fly. If fish dart into plastic rings or gaskets, their gills may be gashed or damaged, causing loss of oxygen and finally death. Seal pups are especially curious and often poke their heads into six-pack rings. Then as the seals grow, the rings become collars or belts of death, choking or squeezing the life out of them.

Sea lions and dolphins often become entangled

Other innocent victims of water pollution: (top) an elephant seal is washed ashore, its neck encased in a metal ring; (bottom) a pelican rests its head on a branch as it tries to free itself from an entangled fishing line.

in the miles of plastic netting that are spread out by commercial fisheries. Even when the nets are abandoned or slip away, they continue to "ghost fish," capturing sea life. Each year an estimated 30,000 sea lions die because of such entanglement.

Plastic bags, sheeting, and gloves in the water resemble jellyfish or other prey to marine wildlife. CMC reported that autopsies revealed one dead turtle with fifteen plastic bags in its stomach, and a dead whale with fifty.

Plastic pellets, the product of synthesizing petrochemicals, are the raw materials that manufacturers melt down to form plastic goods. Frequently, these pellets make their way into the seas. Floating on the waters or washing up on beaches, the pellets look like eggs even to seasoned marine researchers. Seabirds ingest the pellets, as well as other small plastic items, then die of suffocation or intestinal blockage. In one instance, the body of an albatross was found with its flesh decomposed, but the deadly plastic objects it had ingested were still intact.

Is anything being done about the peril of plastics, which some now call floating mines, on the seas? CMC, along with many other environmental groups and governmental agencies such as NOAA, has been distributing brochures and audiovisuals that depict the effects of plastic pollution in the oceans. A number of environmental groups sponsor beach cleanup projects. Volunteers collect and complete information cards on marine debris, which helps in the process of developing a central data bank about sources and types of plastic debris polluting the seas. State and local antilitter campaigns also increase public awareness of plastic pollution.

Manufacturers are finding ways to recycle some plastics, and a few states have set up recycling cen-

*A turtle drags his unwelcome
plastic catch to shore.*

ters for plastic materials. Degradable plastics are also being developed, although there is debate on whether plastics actually break down in ways that do not harm the environment.

Enforcement of national and international laws also is needed to help stem the flow of plastic in the oceans. The U.S. government has ratified an international treaty called the International Convention for the Prevention of Pollution from Ships, shortened to Marine Pollution Convention or MARPOL. One part of the treaty prohibits the disposal of all plastics into the sea. Dumping of other wastes, such as rags, metal, and glass, is also banned less than 12 miles (19 km) from the nearest land. But as CMC put it: "Much more than the force of law will be needed. . . . While the ocean is not big enough to handle the incoming tide of plastics, it is large enough to hide offenders who will continue to dispose of plastics at sea. So, seafarers must be encouraged to dispose of plastic trash at shore-based facilities and such facilities must be convenient and easily accessible."[45]

Although millions of pounds of plastic materials have been dumped into the sea each year and 100,000 tons of plastic fishing gear are lost annually, land sources account for much more of the plastic debris in oceans. As with other contaminants, rivers and streams carry plastic throwaways to the sea. Sewage discharges, beach and dock litter, and industrial wastes discharged into waterways also contribute to plastic in the oceans. Recycling and lower consumer demand for nonessential plastic items have to be part of the overall effort to control the vast amount of plastics polluting the environment.

AWASH IN OIL

Santa Barbara, California, marked a not-so-pleasant anniversary in February 1989. Twenty years earlier, the Union Oil Company was drilling offshore 6 miles (almost 10 km) south of Santa Barbara when oil began to gush from weblike cracks in the ocean floor. For the next twelve days the oil spread far and wide, covering 800 square miles (2,071 sq km) of near-shore waters and beaches, and coating birds, fish, and marine mammals.

Although the gushing oil, called a blowout, did not result in long-term damage to the environment, people in the area were worried about beach degradation. A year before, there had been three oil tanker accidents in the Santa Barbara channel. "The blowout was the straw that broke the camel's back," a Santa Barbara County commissioner told a news reporter. As a result, no oil companies were allowed to lease land for the purpose until 1983.

Another outcome of the Santa Barbara spill was to spur federal legislation protecting coastal areas and marine life. An amendment to the Outer Continental Shelf Leasing Act in 1978 tightened regulations on offshore drilling and set up more strict monitoring of oil company operations.

However, drilling and tanker accidents still occurred. In 1979, for example, an oil well in the Gulf of Mexico blew, causing the world's largest spill. But much of the 140 million gallons (529,900,000 liters) of crude oil disintegrated through the action of bacteria that attack *hydrocarbons* (such as oil). Wind and waves also dispersed the oil in the open sea.

Yet marine scientists warn that oil spills should always be considered disasters. Scientists learned from a 1978 tanker accident in the English Channel

*Drilling for oil in the coastal waters
of Southern California is of concern to
environmentalists who fear "blowouts," or
oil spills that can damage sea life and
plants along the shore.*

just off the coast of France that an oil spill causes immediate and mass killings of sea life and plants and animals on shore. Then the damage continues in a more subtle fashion because of imbalances in the ecological system. After the English Channel spill, many species of birds, fish, and shellfish began to disappear. Scientists expect that it will take decades for the area to recover.

A major scientific study of a spill off the Panamanian coast in 1986 documented the deadly effects of oil slicks that cover marine life. Published in *Science*, the study pointed out that the coastal habitat suffered more damage than had been expected. "After 1.5 years only some organisms in areas exposed to the open sea have recovered," the scientists reported.[46]

Prince William Sound in Alaska may suffer a similar fate. In March 1989, the oil tanker the *Exxon Valdez* ran aground on a reef and spilled nearly 11 million gallons (41,635,000 liters) of crude oil. The huge spill has been called an "ecological massacre." As the oil spread, it covered sea animals, birds, and the shores for hundreds of square miles.

Plankton, kelp, and sea grasses along with shellfish have died, destroying food sources for fish and sea mammals. Some sea animals, such as seals, have starved because of fish losses. Sea otters covered with oil have died from loss of body heat or have starved because of the poisoned food supply. Migrating birds have been unable to find food, and some have not reproduced. Geese and other waterfowl that dive for food have been covered with oil, then have died.

Most ecological experts predict that it will be years before the true extent of damages will be known. Meantime, some government officials called for improvements in the speed and technology with which oil companies handle spills. But hardly had these pronouncements been made when additional oil spills occurred. During one week in June 1989, tankers spilled oil off Rhode Island, Delaware, and in Galveston Bay, Texas. In February 1990, an oil tanker owned by American Trading Transportation Company was attempting to anchor off Huntington Beach, California, to unload its cargo of crude oil. One of the ship's 12-ton anchors punctured a hole in the tanker, spilling 300,000 gallons of oil and threatening coastal wetlands and a wildlife refuge.

Oil spills, wherever and whenever they occur, reflect a bigger issue: the continuing threat of human activities on the fragile web of life in marine ecosystems. As many marine experts have pointed out, we need a better understanding of our ocean resources and how such activities as oil exploration and transportation of crude oil affect the health of the marine environment.

THE GLOBAL SEWER

Oil spills and slicks create crisis situations, but until recently little publicity was given to the vast amounts of sewage, industrial wastes, and *dredgings* from waterways that are dumped regularly from barges and ships into the seas. Most industrialized nations use the Atlantic and the North Sea as major dump sites or for burning hazardous materials in shipboard incinerators.

An international agreement known as the London Dumping Convention (LDC) prohibits the disposal of high-level radioactive wastes and certain toxic substances such as mercury and cadmium compounds in the oceans. But participating nations do not agree on whether low-level radioactive wastes should be dumped or whether hazardous wastes should be incinerated on ships at sea.

According to *The Earth Report*, "In 1984, some 5,570,000 [metric tons] of industrial waste were dumped directly into the North Sea, together with 5,100 [metric tons] of sewage sludge, and 97 million [metric tons] of dredge material." The dumpings, along with other pollutants in the sea, have created what Dutch officials have called "one of the most polluted seas on earth." Holland, West Germany, Belgium, Norway, and Denmark have called for measures to protect the North Sea. But Britain, the only European nation still dumping sewage sludge into the sea, has long argued that no definite scientific evidence links waste dumping with such problems as eutrophication and poisoning of sea life.[47]

Whether they are dumping in the North Sea or other oceans, proponents of such waste disposal insist that sewage and industrial wastes are diluted and dispersed by the vast ocean waters and currents. That argument has been the basis of dumping practices in most coastal areas of the United States. However, Congress banned all ocean dumping in an amendment to the Marine Protection, Research, and Sanctuaries Act (known as the Ocean Dumping Act), which took effect in 1981.

Nevertheless, New York City challenged the law, and the court declared that ocean dumping should be permitted if it does not degrade the marine environment. As a result nine sewer agencies in New York and New Jersey are allowed to dump 5.5 million gallons (20,817,500 liters) of sludge every day at a site on the edge of the continental shelf, 106 miles (170.5 km) east of Cape May, New Jersey.

"For fifty years, the city has disposed of sludge in the Atlantic Ocean without incident," declared former New York mayor Edward Koch in an opinion piece for the *EPA Journal*. "Ocean disposal does not deplete oxygen levels that are needed to sustain marine life. Neither does it introduce toxic concentration of heavy metals or other pollutants into the ocean. Laboratory tests have established that the city's sludge is harmless when diluted by seawater," Koch stated.

But Governor Thomas Kean of New Jersey disagreed, asserting that disposing of sludge in the ocean was "gambling on the unknown." According to Kean's argument, there have been "dramatic advances in pretreatment to remove toxic metals from sludge," and technologies exist to burn sludge safely and to reduce the amount of sludge. Since forty-eight other states use such technologies, including waste disposal systems in most of New York State and southern New Jersey, Governor Kean felt the New York–New Jersey area should do the same. "Ending sludge dumping . . . will show that we appreciate the ocean's value and fragile nature," he wrote.[48]

Beyond appreciation of the marine ecosystem is the fact that ocean researchers have discovered that waste, no matter what type, does not lie undisturbed at the bottom. Instead, violent underwater storms batter the ocean floor and move huge amounts of sediment. Rusting drums of hazardous materials that were once dumped at sea may even now be leaking, and their contents may be scattered by storms.

What about burning hazardous wastes at sea? That is an issue that also creates great controversy. Some experts say that ocean incineration is safe and that it is the most cost-effective way to dispose of the more that 50 million metric tons of hazardous wastes that are generated each year in the United States alone. When modern incineration equipment is used and burning is handled correctly, all but about .0001 of the material is destroyed. But at best that can result in a ton of waste left over after burning 10,000 tons.

Opponents of ocean incineration point out that even small amounts of unburned hazardous wastes can accumulate in marine organisms. Another danger of burning hazardous wastes at sea is the possibility that, like an oil tanker, an incineration ship could suffer an accident and leak, which could be a major catastrophe. The EPA warned that less than half a ship's cargo of PCBs would not only contaminate the upper part of the Gulf of Mexico but also deteriorate all life in the Gulf.

There are no simple answers to the problem of hazardous waste disposal, whether on land or at sea. But one part of the solution is to stem the sources of hazardous waste.

CHAPTER EIGHT
WHEN WELLS, RIVERS, AND LAKES GO DRY

On the Mississippi River, barges loaded with cargo are stranded because of low water levels. In the Midwest, corn shrivels and dies after weeks of hot weather and no rain. In southern California, where rainfall has been low for years, a reservoir dries up leaving only cracked earth. In an area of Florida where groundwater has been depleted, a sinkhole suddenly opens up and swallows a house. On the Great Plains, extended drought dries up prairie potholes, and ducks cannot find food or refuge. In Georgia, boat docks on a lake that supplies Atlanta's water stand high and dry because of several successive dry years.

In many parts of the United States, droughts and heavy demands on freshwater sources make it even more important to protect the quality of available water sources. But that is no simple task, as is clear from the varied and interrelated water pollution problems that must be overcome. In addition, people usually take water resources for granted until supplies are threatened or cut back.

MANAGING WATER RESOURCES

Added to the problems of cleaning up water supplies is the increasingly difficult task of managing water resources so that they are distributed where needed and used efficiently. During the early part of the 1900s, managing U.S. water resources usually meant building dams and irrigation systems. Under the direction of the federal Bureau of Reclamation, and with the help of the Army Corps of Engineers, billions of dollars' worth of projects were completed to control rivers and turn deserts into productive farmland.

Today many environmental groups and members of Congress oppose building new dams and irrigation projects. Not only are costs prohibitive, but existing dams and irrigation systems have caused environmental problems. Silt deposits build up in the reservoirs behind dams, sometimes reducing water supplies by 50 percent. When there is large-scale irrigation of land, soils become saline, too salty for crops or pasture.

Although salinization occurs in both irrigated and nonirrigated lands, irrigation tends to speed up the process. In areas with abundant rainfall, salts are washed out of soils. But in semiarid or arid regions, salts remain in soils and are leached out with the flow of irrigation water, leaving a white crust on top. Irrigation water may also transport salts into groundwater and eventually into rivers and streams, thus creating saline conditions for water downstream, which also may be drawn for irrigation purposes.

Projects to prevent soil salinity, which affects about 23 percent of U.S. cropland and pastureland, is part of water resource management today. In fact, it is essential in arid regions where crop production depends almost entirely on effective irrigation.

"Irrigated agriculture accounts for more than 40 percent of all freshwater withdrawals in the United States and consumes nearly three times as much water as all other uses combined," the U.S. Department of Agriculture reported.[49] The vast amount of water used for irrigation has created intense competition for supplies, particularly in the West. As populations continue to grow in such states as California, Arizona, Colorado, and Texas, some communities will not have enough water to provide for both agricultural and urban needs.

Complex water rights are at the root of some supply problems. In the East, landowners have riparian rights—the right to use water that flows through their property; if the water is diverted it must be used for "reasonable and beneficial" purposes and then be allowed to flow back to its source.

Land ownership is not the basis for western water rights. Water laws are based on what is called "prior appropriation doctrine." It is first come, first served—those who first use the water for a beneficial purpose can claim the rights to it, and those rights are passed on to descendants. However, if the water is not used, rights to it are forfeited. At the same time the federal government, through the Bureau of Reclamation, has rights to some water sources (such as reservoirs at federal dams) and provides water for many western farmers at very low rates.

STRETCHING WATER RESOURCES

In some regions, a variety of federal agencies, state water districts, regional and municipal water companies, and private individuals have some claim on water resources. Along California's south coast in Santa Barbara County, for example, eighteen major water agencies and 170 smaller private and public companies provide water for agricultural and urban county use. About 85 percent of the supply comes from groundwater, which is being withdrawn faster than it can be replenished. Several thousand individual landowners also pump water from underground sources. But, as a *Santa Barbara News-Press* series in 1989 noted, water purveyors seldom work together, and a shortage of water in the county has created controversy over how to increase supplies.

Conservation is one way to stretch supplies and is touted throughout Santa Barbara County and the state. Water purveyors regularly reward those who conserve. In one case, a water company honored a resident who had cut her household water consumption nearly in half with various water-saving devices. The company landscaped the customer's yard free of charge, using drought-resistant plants that require much less water than a grass lawn.

Water companies often post ideas for voluntary conservation. Among the recommendations: take shorter showers, repair leaking toilets, and don't let the water run continuously while cleaning vegetables, washing dishes, brushing teeth, or shaving. Using an automatic dishwasher or washing machine only for a full load is one more helpful conservation measure.

However, voluntary conservation can be difficult to maintain if most residents in a community do not cooperate. Some companies add fines to water bills when customers use more than allotted amounts of water during times of drought. But fines mean very little to those who can afford the cost. At least fifty wealthy property owners with huge estates in Santa Barbara County have paid annual fines ranging from $12,000 to $32,000.

[105]

A shadow across the billboard appears to mark the line between northern and Southern California, and the words clearly point up the problem: Water is scarce in Southern California. A variety of conservation measures and efforts to increase water resources are under way in the state.

Water use on an 18-acre (7-hectare) estate owned by Texas financier Harold Simmons was estimated at more than 10 million gallons (about 38 million liters) in 1988, enough water to supply a family of five for thirty-one years. The water was used primarily to keep lawns, shrubs, and other plants green and growing. Even though the county suffered a water shortage, Simmons refused to cut back. "Why should I?" he wanted to know, adding that as long as he was willing to pay the price, he should be able to keep his grass green. Simmons seems to personify an old saying about water in the West: it does not flow downhill; it flows toward money.

Nevertheless, some estate owners in the area have reduced water consumption, and water experts continue to look for other ways to increase supplies. Some believe that Lake Cachuma, a major water reservoir created by a dam, should be enlarged. Others have suggested building more dams and reservoirs. But as with dam projects in other parts of the nation, costs would be extremely high. In addition, more-stringent laws now require that the surrounding environment and endangered wildlife species be protected should dam construction take place.

Santa Barbara County also is stretching its water resources by reclaiming waste water. Some treated waste water is allowed to percolate into aquifers, and some park areas are being irrigated with reclaimed water. During the rainy season, runoff from streets is captured in a system of drains and ponds and also is being used to replenish groundwater.

Desalinization is another possible, albeit expensive, method for increasing Santa Barbara water supplies. Various technologies are available to turn ocean water into potable water, and several private desalinization plants are operating successfully in the county. Such plants also supply potable water to people in other areas of the world, including Kuwait on the Persian Gulf, a Caribbean island, and an island in the English Channel.

One more possible source of water is the State Water Project which supplies many southern California communities. The water is piped from state-operated water reservoirs in northern California. However, in 1989, a third straight year of drought, state officials planned major reductions of water supplies to many cities and towns in southern California and imposed water rationing on northern communities. The Bureau of Reclamation, which supplies about 6.5 million acre-feet to Californians, also planned to reduce supplies by up to 50 percent.

OBSTACLES TO CONSERVATION

Forced reductions in water use and voluntary conservation may be some of the most effective ways to alleviate water shortages. But conservation on a broad scale still faces many obstacles. One is the low cost of water in some parts of the United States. When people do not have to pay high rates for the use of municipal water, they seldom worry about leaking pipes or dripping faucets; there is little incentive to cut back on water use. New York City, which consumes 1.5 billion gallons of water per day and would like to increase to 2 bgd, installed water meters in city buildings for the first time during the summer of 1988.

In western states, water is even less expensive than in the East. As a result, huge quantities of water are used to develop green lawns, golf courses, and parkways and to grow plants and trees that thrive best in areas with regular precipitation. Less water would be consumed if landscaping included more plants and lawn covers native to arid lands. A campaign is under way in Arizona, for example, to encourage residents to use cactus and other desert plants for landscaping purposes.

Another obstacle to conservation is the type of food and fiber crops that are grown in arid regions. Crops such as rice and alfalfa for cattle feed are produced more efficiently in areas with plenty of water. But because water is cheap and western water rights require that water be used, large quantities of rice and other "thirsty" crops are grown on land that has to be irrigated.

Marc Reisner, author of *Cadillac Desert*, noted that during 1986 "just under a million acres of California cropland were planted in grass" to feed cows and sheep, which required "4.2 million acre-feet of water—the domestic consumption, including swimming pools and lawns, of 22 million people."[50] The irony is that pastureland provides only a small portion of California's annual income. Since more than half the states in the nation grow pasture using only rainwater, California's meat and dairy products could be produced elsewhere and shipped to the coast at a lower cost.

However, even if farmers wanted to shift from growing pasture to producing oranges, lemons, grapes, or other food crops that require less water, the appropriative rights doctrine would discourage such a change. Since water rights are granted on the basis of "beneficial use" (in this case, the need for large quantities of water to produce feed for cattle and sheep), farmers who switched to growing fruit crops would lose the rights to water they did not need.

In the Plains region, farmers also have been encouraged to increase groundwater use because of various agricultural policies. Many farmers grow cotton, which needs to be irrigated, and receive price support payments for the crop because it is a surplus commodity and thus sells at a low price. Other farm subsidies, such as payments for crops that fail, also destroy incentives to conserve water. Another disincentive is a special deduction on federal income taxes. As geology professor Donald Coates explained: " . . . farmers are granted a depletion allowance on pumped groundwater, thereby enjoying a tax break similar to that the oil industry had for many years and the mineral industry currently enjoys. Thus the more water that is pumped and consumed, the less tax that must be paid." [51]

As a result of such policies and the fact that farmers prosper with large irrigated acreage, the Ogallala aquifer, which provides water for the Plains region, is greatly overdrawn. About the size of California, the Ogallala underlies a major portion of Nebraska, and parts of Kansas, Oklahoma, Colorado, New Mexico, and Texas. The region is one of the richest agricultural areas in the world, producing more than $15 billion in products annually. At least 150,000 (perhaps up to 200,000) irrigation wells draw water from the aquifer. Each year about 21 million acre-feet of groundwater are pumped, but only about 1 million acre-feet are replaced annually. As the water is depleted, land is lost to productive agriculture. If current trends continue, the region will lose up to 5 million acres (more than 2 million hectares) of irrigated land by the year 2005.

During the past decade there have been a number of proposals for importing water to the Plains region. One plan called for tapping into Canadian water supplies and sending it south at a cost of over $100 billion. The plan, like several other water transfer schemes over the past decade, has been dropped. Instead, conservation still seems to be one of the few workable methods for protecting groundwater supplies.

Some Plains farmers are converting to water-saving irrigation methods. Traditionally, to irrigate large fields, farmers have flooded furrows between rows of crops or used large mobile sprinkling systems. But up to 50 percent of the water in furrows runs off and does not get used by the plants. A more expensive drip irrigation method, but one that uses much less water, is being adopted by some farmers. In drip irrigation, water hoses or pipes drip water only at the base of plants, allowing most of the water to reach the roots. More farmers are also planting crops that need less moisture.

Another effort to conserve water in the Plains is the Conservation Reserve Program. The federal government pays farmers $40 to $50 per acre (about 0.4 hectares) each year for land set aside for erosion control. The acreage must be planted in trees or plants that hold soil in place, and cannot be used for crop production for ten years. Even though the land can be returned to productive use, farmers must meet strict conservation measures if they plan to apply for crop subsidies.

Yet a number of water experts believe that water shortages in some regions will continue and that people will be forced to cut back. Even if resources are stretched with various conservation methods or new sources of water are found, developing and distributing supplies will be increasingly expensive. In short, experts say, the cost of water will rise and people will use less.

CHAPTER NINE

PROTECTIVE MEASURES

After all the discussion of endangered water resources, it appears at times that the quality of water for drinking and other purposes has been irreversibly damaged. But even heavily contaminated waters can be cleaned up. If pollutants no longer enter a waterway or waterbody, the system usually can recover. But ultimately people have to work together in a variety of ways to make sure that our common water supplies are protected.

On a global scale, world leaders have held a number of conferences over the past two decades to deal with worldwide environmental problems, many of which are the result of economic expansion. In developed nations, there are a number of critics who rail against so-called Third World countries that are consuming natural resources at a rapid rate in order to meet the basic needs of growing populations. With 800 million people worldwide still living in absolute poverty, it is difficult to see how the haves of the world can tell the have-nots to stop trying to make economic gains.

In 1983, the United Nations set up the World Commission on Environment and Development to try to deal with the complex, interrelated issues of economic growth and preservation of the environment. Gro Harlem Brundtland, chairman of the commission and prime minister of Norway, believes that economic growth in developing countries is the primary way to eliminate poverty, but she wrote: "We cannot treat the atmosphere, soils, water, and oceans as sinks for the by-products of human activities. Growth must enhance the environment rather than degrade it. Growth must be distributed in an equitable manner among and within countries."

To that end, Brundtland would like to see a global ethic developed "which recognizes that there are limits to what we can do to the environment. . . . Environmental concerns must become an integral part of decision-making at all levels." The commissioner believes that executives in business communities around the world are beginning to see that technology that does not harm the environment is a benefit to business and provides "a competitive edge."[52]

ENVIRONMENTAL LAWS

In the United States, some businesses certainly have been trying to provide a safe environment while maintaining a strong economy. Yet rules and regulations also are important in determining whether the environment will be protected, particularly when there are concerns about company profits or keeping jobs in a community. Past practices usually have favored immediate economic benefits, not the environment.

At the federal level, a number of environmental laws have been enacted since the 1960s to protect water and other natural resources. President Lyndon B. Johnson signed the Water Quality Act of 1965, which was supposed to ensure clean waterways by the year 2000. But another major federal law protecting water supplies had to be passed just seven years later. The U.S. Clean Water Act of 1972 (CWA) set standards for water quality and prohibited the flow of industrial wastes and municipal sewage into waterways. At the same time, CWA provided funds for cities to modernize their outmoded sewage treatment plants.

Canada also passed a federal statute in 1972, called the Canada Water Act, in response to public calls for protection of North American waterways. Similar to the U.S. law, the Canadian statute banned various industrial pollutants and set standards for sewage treatment. But Canada went a step further and completely banned detergent phosphates, which were partly responsible for the nutrient overload and eutrophication of some of the waters of the Great Lakes. Canadian provincial laws, along with U.S. state and municipal laws passed in the 1970s, also helped protect freshwater sources, even though soap companies, steel industries, and other manufacturers fought bans on industrial wastes discharged into waterways.

In 1974, the U.S. Safe Drinking Water Act gave the Environmental Protection Agency authority to set limits for any contaminants in drinking water that would be a threat to public health. Amendments were made to the Clean Water Act that granted the EPA authority to control pollutants in groundwater. Other federal laws, although set up to protect various natural resources, have an impact on water supplies. For example, the Resource Conservation and Recovery Act, the Toxic Substances Control Act, and the Hazardous Materials Transportation Act were passed to regulate the transport and disposal of hazardous waste.

The Soil and Water Resources Conservation Act of 1977 called for a National Conservation Program (NCP), which was established in 1982 under the direction of the U.S. Department of Agriculture. Some of the goals of the NCP are to reduce excessive soil erosion and agricultural nonpoint source pollution of water, improve irrigation efficiency, and promote more-effective use of water.

A variety of U.S. laws and international treaties passed during the 1970s help protect ocean waters and sea life. The U.S. Marine Mammal Protection Act of 1972, for example, was designed to reduce the deaths of porpoises caught in the huge nets used in commercial tuna fishing. The Marine Protection, Research, and Sanctuaries Act protects marine areas off U.S. coasts in a way similar to how national forests and parks are preserved. The map in Figure 5 shows the various locations of sanctuaries set up by the National Oceanic and Atmospheric Administration's Marine Sanctuary program. Along with laws that prohibit disposal of plastics in the ocean, other federal legislation regulates the transport of hazardous materials through ports and sets up measures to protect coastal waters.

States also have passed laws to protect water resources. Maine, Massachusetts, Rhode Island, and North Carolina are just a few states that enacted legislation during the 1960s to preserve coastal wetlands. Other states followed during the 1970s. In efforts to protect groundwater, state and local ordinances have been enacted to control specific

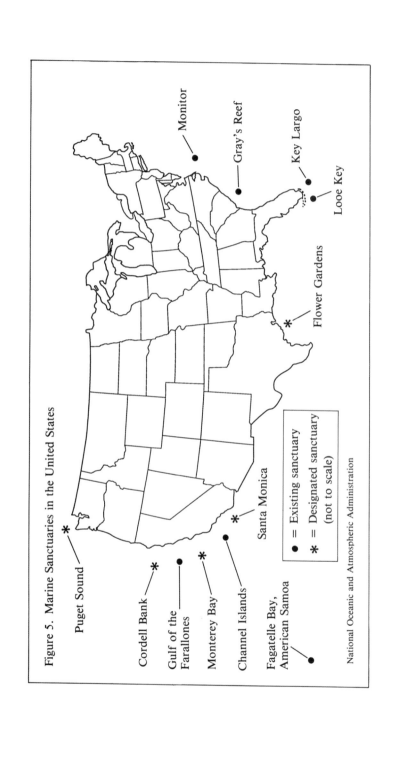

Figure 5. Marine Sanctuaries in the United States

Monitor

Gray's Reef

Key Largo

Looe Key

Flower Gardens

Puget Sound

Cordell Bank

Gulf of the Farallones

Monterey Bay

Channel Islands

Santa Monica

Fagatelle Bay, American Samoa

● = Existing sanctuary

* = Designated sanctuary (not to scale)

National Oceanic and Atmospheric Administration

sources of contamination, such as underground storage tanks and discharge of toxic substances from industries.

One regulatory program has been set up in California with enactment of the Safe Drinking Water and Toxic Enforcement Act. Better known as Proposition 65, the law went into effect in 1988 and requires businesses to warn of exposure to toxic chemicals used in products or released into the air and water. The warning provision created a great deal of controversy because it requires industry to use labels and signs to alert the public of possible cancer and reproductive dangers of certain chemicals rather than requiring regulatory agencies to make the case.

Proposition 65 also deals with pesticides that run off into streams, a major source of nonpoint pollutants. However, agricultural runoff in California and other states is difficult to control, as has been pointed out in previous chapters. "Today just 9 percent of stream pollution comes from industry. Fully 65 percent is nonpoint, primarily from agriculture," wrote Contributing Editor Gregg Easterbrook in a special report for *Newsweek*. Easterbrook went on to explain that "The EPA has authority to certify pesticides but little ability to restrict their use to prevent runoff pollution; Congress . . . has been gun-shy about the link between agricultural chemicals and pollution."[53]

COOPERATIVE EFFORTS

Even though legal controls on pesticides and other agricultural chemicals may be difficult to enforce, a variety of state and local programs were established in the late 1970s and during the 1980s to deal with runoff that contaminates water supplies. Most of the programs have been part of the NCP, which is coordinating the work of various federal, state, and local agencies, and is enlisting voluntary action by farmers.

Demonstration projects have convinced some landowners of the value of "best management practices." Of course what is "best" for one farm may not be appropriate for another.

In Iowa, noted for the production of corn, soybeans, cattle, and hogs, farmers have used millions of pounds of herbicides, insecticides, and nitrogen fertilizers on crops and pastureland. This heavy use of agricultural chemicals apparently has resulted in nitrate contamination of groundwater and "detectable levels" of pesticides in public water supplies that come from surface water. Although most farmers do not advocate eliminating all agrochemicals, many have cut back on their use. As one farmer put it: "The chemicals we use could affect our own drinking water . . . [but] we're caught between an economic and environmental issue here. Drink contaminated water, and you could be hurt; lose the farm [because of low yields], and you will be hurt."[54]

Some farmers have turned to no-till methods. In no-till farming, the residue of the harvested crop (corn for example) is left on the unplowed land and a new crop such as soybeans is planted in rows through the residue. This can greatly reduce the use of chemical pesticides and prevent soil erosion, which lead to contamination of water supplies.

Because pesticides often kill "good bugs"—those that feed on pests—along with the "bad bugs," some farmers have been using another agricultural practice that reduces or eliminates the need for pesticides. Called biological control or integrated pest management, beneficial insects are introduced into fields or orchards to feed on pests that destroy crops.

More than a century ago, vast numbers of vedalia beetles (ladybugs) were released into California orange groves to eat a destructive scale on the trees, and the ladybugs have helped prevent economic damage from the scale ever since. In recent years, biocontrol has helped farmers and ranchers around the world use predators that naturally destroy insect and weed pests. Wolf spiders prey naturally on brown planthoppers, which have destroyed millions of tons of rice in Asian countries. Ladybugs have controlled aphids—lice that draw sap from plants— in France, China, Germany, England, and the United States. Several species of stingless wasps have been used in parts of the United States to control weevils that have caused great damage to alfalfa crops.

"ATTACK BUGS" AND OTHER CLEANUP METHODS

Scientists also are using "attack bugs"—microbes— to feed on contaminants in water, a process called *bioremediation*. Microbiologists have been experimenting with species of bacteria that are native to aquifers and can break down hydrocarbons such as oil and gasoline in groundwater and soil. Bacteria convert hydrocarbons to *carbon dioxide* and methane gases, which are released to the atmosphere. However, bacteria work slowly underground, so the scientists have found ways to speed up the process. They pump fluids that contain high concentrations of oxygen and nutrients into the soil, which in turn prompt the microbes to "gorge themselves."[55]

In one instance, Stanford University scientists

used bacteria to clean up an aquifer underlying Mountain View, California. The groundwater was contaminated with TCE, *vinyl chloride*, and other chemicals that had leaked from semiconductor plants. Scientists pumped oxygen and methane into the aquifer, which helped the microbes produce enzymes that "ate" the chemicals, leaving harmless by-products such as salt.

To protect groundwater at a Los Angeles site, microbes cleaned up oil that had leaked from underground storage tanks. In another instance, "bugs" in waste water destroyed chemicals used in wood-preserving processes. In the future, bacteria may also be used to degrade PCBs in river sediments and pesticides in soils and waterways. [56]

Another experiment has been under way at the University of California at Riverside to use fungi on irrigation waters that have washed toxic selenium into wetlands, poisoning waterfowl and other wildlife. In laboratory tests, several attack fungi have converted selenium to a harmless gas that washes away.

Bioremediation does not work on all contaminants in water supplies, and other methods of cleansing the water may be more appropriate or just as effective. In areas where soils are contaminated with nitrates that seep into private wells, people may choose to dig deeper wells and install filter systems in their homes. Some contaminants may have to be pumped from the wells, called purge wells, and run through carbon filters, then returned to the ground through storm sewers.

Contaminants also can be removed with air-stripping towers, a method sometimes used to cleanse municipal water supplies. Basically, water is pumped into the top of the towers, which can range from 15 to 100 feet (4.6 to 30.5 m) high, and air is pumped into the bottom. Pollutants evaporate into the air, and the air flows through carbon filters before it is released.

CONTROLLING INDUSTRIAL TOXINS

Of course it would be the best of all worlds if no toxic compounds were produced in the first place. But most consumers today, including the majority of Americans and people in other industrialized nations as well as developing countries, want more and more manufactured goods. And manufacturing processes release toxic wastes from factories into the air, land, or water, thereby increasing pollution. Few people would opt to return to the days of no machinery, no engine-driven vehicles, or no electric power and the vast array of products that depend on electricity. So how can industrial wastes that may contain poisonous materials be eliminated?

Some manufacturers have been trying to eliminate hazardous materials in finished products—producing biodegradable paper and plastics, for example, or using a variety of methods to detoxify wastes before releasing them into the environment. A few companies have installed waste water treatment facilities that discharge almost potable water into streams or oceans. Other manufacturers are experimenting with bioremediation, using microbes to break down toxic materials.

Other methods for reducing toxic materials in water supplies include better incineration—facilities that burn wastes rather than releasing them into waterways but that burn them so that the release of toxic gases into the atmosphere is prevented. Some companies recycle materials, such as solvents, that had previously been waste. Ink solvents can be recovered and reused, as an example. A number of companies are using water-based printing inks so that they can clean their presses with water instead of hazardous solvents.

Old-fashioned soap-and-water cleaning has replaced the use of cleaning solvents in other industries. Scrubbers are used instead of solvents in one 3M plant. Using rotating brushes rather than toxic chemicals to clean electronic circuits does the job effectively without producing hazardous waste.

EDUCATIONAL PROGRAMS

Although protective measures are not as widely applied as many people would like, the problem of cleaning up water supplies and keeping them clean also requires an understanding of what our water resources are and how each person can play a part in conserving water and reducing contaminants. That is the goal of a variety of educational programs in schools and for community groups. Many educational projects are sponsored by state departments of natural resources, environmental departments, or departments of education. Sometimes a science teacher or other staff member will conduct a class project on the environment. In some urban areas, projects have included continual cleanup of harbors or streams, studies of how sewage disposal systems work, and career education with emphasis on professions related to the environment.

In some states, environmental education is an important part of the school curriculum. California has one of the most extensive statewide education programs on the environment, particularly stressing water resources. In recent years, curriculum guides have been prepared to teach middle-grade and junior high students about marine resources, water conservation, and protecting water supplies.

One recent project under way in Santa Barbara County, California, is sponsored in part by the National Oceanic and Atmospheric Administration's National Marine Sanctuary program. Students can learn basic oceanographic concepts in an outdoor Pier Lab, set up on Santa Barbara's Stearns Wharf, which is a major tourist center as well as a commercial fishing wharf. The Pier Lab consists of several hands-on learning stations where students learn about the biology and physical properties of the ocean and about marine ecology.

At the biology station, for example, students tow in plankton nets that have been dropped alongside the pier and then place their samples under a microscope-camera system that projects the enlarged image of the plankton into a color monitor. Laboratory staff explain the process of *photosynthesis* and the concept of food chains. At other Pier Lab stations, students see demonstrations of how oceanographers gather data on water visibility and temperature, observe settling plates that show how marine larvae develop, and get acquainted with various sea creatures by holding them.

Across the nation on the East Coast, a number of projects in Pennsylvania, Maryland, and Virginia inform students and community groups about improving the quality of water in the Chesapeake Bay, the nation's largest estuary, which has been greatly damaged over the past few decades. More than 15 million people live along the rivers and creeks that empty into the bay and in port cities and shore communities. Increasing population and growing commercial, industrial, and recreational activities in the

Bay Area put great pressure on the estuary's fragile ecology. Rivers carry heavy sediment loads, a major pollutant, into the bay, and toxic materials in waste discharges continue to accumulate and destroy fish and shellfish. Oyster harvests, as one example, have fallen from an average annual yield of 2 to 3 million bushels to 800,000 bushels.

Restoration of the Chesapeake Bay was declared a national priority in the mid-1980s, and the three Bay States plus the District of Columbia joined to do something about cleaning it up. Laws have been passed and funds have been provided to address pollution problems. At the same time civic groups such as the Citizens Program for the Chesapeake Bay, the Chesapeake Bay Foundation, Save Our Streams, and government agencies of the Bay States are working together to educate citizens about their roles in preserving the bay.

A major cooperative project has been the publication of the *Baybook*, a guide for reducing water pollution at home and in a community.* The guide, published in late 1987, has been distributed free of charge and is not copyrighted so that the information can reach as many people as possible.

---

* Limited copies of the *Baybook* are available from the Alliances for the Chesapeake Bay, Inc., 6600 York Road, Baltimore, MD 21212.

CHAPTER TEN

TAKING ACTION

Educational programs not only have helped to heighten awareness of water pollution hazards but often have prompted action. In some cases, it may be a local campaign to collect and safely dispose of leftover household products that could contaminate waterways. Seashore and riverbank cleanup projects are common ways that community groups act to restore the quality of their local water resources. In other instances, individuals may need to take action. That is often the case when contaminants have entered a drinking water supply or when there is a potential danger to underground or surface waters used for household purposes.

SHOULD YOU DRINK THE WATER?

How do people know when the quality of their drinking water is endangered? In some cases, a change in the taste, odor, or color might warn them of water contamination. But most hazardous pollutants are not easily recognized, and the only way to find out about the quality of water is to have it tested in a laboratory. People who use private wells should have their water tested regularly, checking for nitrates and pathogens. If you live near an industrial site, landfill, dry cleaning plant, paint shop, or other facilities that might discharge or leak toxic materials into water supplies, a water test would be advisable.

A danger for people living in older homes is the possibility that lead might leach into plumbing lines. In 1986, federal law banned the use of lead in household plumbing systems, but many older buildings have lead pipes or lead-based solder has been used to weld the joints in copper pipes. Since lead is a soft metal, it may dissolve as water flows through the pipes.

Most municipal water supplies meet the Environmental Protection Agency's drinking water standards, but because of the dangers posed by older plumbing systems, the EPA requires municipal water companies to inform their customers of "potential adverse health effects of lead" in drinking water. Lead poisoning in young children can retard mental and physical development, and in adults can cause high blood pressure and damage to the nervous system and kidneys. In many communities, water companies have been sending out informative leaflets with water bills, explaining how lead might enter the water supply.

If you or anyone in your family suspects that your drinking water contains lead, the experts advise letting the water run for several minutes to flush the line. Cold water should be used for drinking and cooking, since hot water tends to leach more lead than cold water. The best precaution, as with other suspected contaminants, is having the water tested. Officials in the public health department or a department of environmental resources in your community usually can arrange for water testing or suggest private testing laboratories.

If you would like to read more about water testing, detailed advice is included in the July 1988 issue of *Consumer's Research,* published by an independent research group and available in most public libraries. The issue also contains information about water purifiers that can be installed in homes. Purifiers do not remove lead or other metals and inorganic chemicals, but can trap some hazardous organic chemicals.

Because of concerns about the quality of their drinking water, an increasing number of people are buying bottled water. Not all bottled water is free of contaminants, however, and despite the claims on labels may not be any better in quality than the tap water in most homes. It is also "as vulnerable to contamination as tap water."[57] Still, tests have shown that most brands of bottled water are safe to drink.

STEWARDSHIP

Along with immediate efforts to assure a safe drinking water supply at home, there are many other actions that individuals and families can take to protect water resources. Some of the organizations listed at the end of this book in the section titled "Agencies and Organizations" will on request provide you with suggestions for what you can do. A few of their suggestions have been summarized or adapted to include here:

- Use household products that do not contaminate water supplies. Baking soda, for example, is an effective cleaner and contains no hazardous chemicals.

- Take unwanted hazardous household chemicals to a community hazardous waste disposal site or sanitary landfill. Motor oil and antifreeze can go to a gas station with a recycling program. If no disposal or recycling programs are under way in your community, organize a group or suggest that a group begin these efforts.
- Conserve water whenever you can. Drips, leaks, and letting water run continuously while doing household chores can waste large quantities of water.
- For a garden, use fertilizers carefully and according to instructions, or start your own compost pile with vegetable scraps, leaves, and grass. Use insecticides sparingly; wash some pests away with water or insecticidal soap; introduce natural predators that will eat pests. Some examples: ladybugs, lacewings, praying mantises, garter snakes, and toads.
- At the beach or while boating, throw plastic and other debris in waste containers, not in the water or on the land.
- Organize or take part in a project to clean up debris from a stream and its banks or a lake or ocean shore.
- Write or call elected officials in your community or state about polluted water resources or potential hazards to water supplies.
- Support local, state, or national groups working for the preservation of water resources or contact them for guidelines on what you can do in your community or home.

One of the most important actions to undertake is basic to all others—developing the habit of conservation and preservation. Frequently, it's called stewardship, caring for natural resources and using them wisely. What you do may seem minor when you think about the larger community, state, nation, and the world. But each person's daily routine has some impact on the environment, which in turn can affect common water resources. The point is to consider the big picture, *think globally*—but *begin action locally*, in your own community, backyard, or home.

AGENCIES AND ORGANIZATIONS

Center for Marine Conservation
1725 DeSales Street, NW
Washington, DC 20036

Dow Chemical Company
Plastics Public Affairs Department
2040 Willard H. Dow Center
Midland, MI 48674

Environmental Defense Fund
1616 P Street, NW, Suite 150
Washington, DC 20036

Friends of the Earth
530 7th Street, SE
Washington, DC 20003

Greenpeace USA
1436 U Street, NW
Washington, DC 20009

Izaac Walton League of America
1701 North Fort Myer Drive, Suite 1100
Arlington, VA 22209

National Audubon Society
801 Pennsylvania Avenue, SE, Suite 301
Washington, DC 20003

National Fisheries Institute
2000 M Street, NW, Suite 580
Washington, DC 20036

National Oceanic and
Atmospheric Administration
U.S. Department of Commerce
Room 5807
Washington, DC 20230

National Resources Defense Council
1350 New York Avenue, NW, 3rd floor
Washington, DC 20005

National Wildlife Federation
1400 16th Street, NW
Washington, DC 20036

Nature Conservancy
1815 North Lynn Street, Suite 800
Arlington, VA 22209

Oceanic Society
1536 16th Street, NW
Washington, DC 20036

Sierra Club
408 C Street, NW
Washington, DC 20005

Soil Conservation Service
U.S. Department of Agriculture
Room 5105, South Building
Washington, DC 20250

Sport Fishing Institute
1010 Massachusetts Avenue, NW, Suite 100
Washington, DC 20001

U.S. Environmental Protection Agency
401 M Street, SW
Washington, DC 20460

Worldwatch Institute
1776 Massachusetts Avenue, NW
Washington, DC 20036

World Wildlife Fund
1250 24th Street, NW
Washington, DC 20037

SOURCE NOTES

Chapter One: Decades of Dirty Water

1. Armin Maywald, et al., "Water Fit to Drink?", in *The Earth Report* (London: Mitchell Beazley Publishers, 1988; Los Angeles: Price Stern Sloan, 1988), p. 80.
2. Alexander H. Benjamin, "The Letter C No Longer Stands for Courage in Chemistry," *Vital Speeches of the Day*, December 15, 1988 (vol. 55, no. 5), p. 156.
3. United States Department of Agriculture, *The Second RCA Appraisal Soil, Water, and Related Resources on Nonfederal Land in the United States Analysis of Condition and Trends*, Review Draft, July–August 1987, Water Supply and Use Data, section 16, pp. 1–3.
4. United States Environmental Protection Agency, *National Water Quality Inventory 1986 Report to Congress*, pp. 4–5.
5. William Ashworth, *The Late, Great Lakes* (Detroit: Wayne State University Press, 1987), p. 130.
6. "Clean Water: Adding Up the Balance Sheet," *U.S. News & World Report*, February 16, 1987, p. 22.
7. Jack Lewis. "Environmental Problems: The Situation." *EPA Journal*, November/December 1988, p. 27.

Chapter Two: Threats to Groundwater

8. Conservation Foundation, *Groundwater Protection*, a report of the National Groundwater Policy Forum, p. 9.
9. Larry Fruhling. "Please Don't Drink the Water," *The Progressive*, October 1986, p. 32.
10. Conservation Foundation, p. 105.
11. Edward Goldsmith and Nicholas Hildyard (editors), *The Earth Report* (London: Mitchell Beazley Publishers; Los Angeles: Price Stern Sloan, 1988), p. 230.
12. Conservation Foundation, pp. 71–74.

13. Environmental Protection Agency, *Protecting Our Ground Water* (brochure).
14. Armin Maywald, et al. "Water Fit to Drink?" *The Earth Report*. (London: Mitchell Beazley Publishers; Los Angeles: Price Stern Sloan, 1988), pp. 80–83.
15. John Seymour and Herbert Girardet, *Blueprint for a Green Planet* (New York: Prentice-Hall Press, 1987; London: Darling Kindersley Ltd., 1987), pp. 40–49.
16. David Stamps, "The Real Price of Road Salt." *National Wildlife*, December/January 1989, p. 28.
17. Donald R. Coates, *Geology and Society* (New York and London: Chapman and Hall, 1985), p. 88.

Chapter Three: Waste Water Problems

18. U.S. Department of Agriculture, *The Second RCA Appraisal Soil, Water, and Related Resources on Nonfederal Land in the United States Analysis of Condition and Trends*, Review Draft, July/August 1987, Water Supply and Use Data, section 16, p. 8.
19. Wesley Marx, "Swamped by Our Own Sewage," *Reader's Digest*, January 1988, pp. 123–128.
20. John R. Sheaffer and Leonard A. Stevens, *Future Water*. (New York: William Morrow, 1983), pp. 95–106.

Chapter Four: Vital Links—Wetlands

21. United States Environmental Protection Agency, *America's Wetlands: Our Vital Link Between Land and Water* (booklet) (February 1988), p. 2.
22. Council on Environmental Quality, *Environmental Quality, The Seventeenth Annual Report*, pp. 73–74.
23. Environmental Protection Agency, *National Water Quality Inventory, 1986 Report to Congress* (November 1987), p. 84.
24. Donald R. Coates, *Geology and Society* (New York and London: Chapman and Hall, 1985), p. 286.
25. Environmental Protection Agency, *America's Wetlands: Our Vital Link Between Land and Water* (booklet) (February 1988), p. 8.
26. Ibid.

Chapter Five: Scum Green and Ice Blue Lakes

27. Environmental Protection Agency, *National Water Quality Inventory, 1986 Report to Congress* (November 1987), p. 34.
28. Ibid., p. 32.

[133]

29. Ibid., pp. 36–38.
30. William Ashworth. *The Late, Great Lakes* (Detroit: Wayne State University Press, 1987), p. 185.
31. Deborah S. Snavely, "Great Lakes Water-Use Date Base—Planning for the 21st Century," *United States Geological Survey Yearbook, Fiscal Year 1987*, p. 98.
32. Ray Formaknek, Jr. (Associated Press Writer), "Research Links Acid Rain to Mercury Levels in Midwest Fish," *South Bend Tribune*, March 9, 1986, p. B2.

Chapter Six: Trouble in River City

33. Michael Riley, "Dead Cats, Toxins and Typhoid," *Time*, April 20, 1987, p. 69.
34. Richard A. Smith, et al. "Water-Quality Trends in the Nation's Rivers." *Science*, March 27, 1987, pp. 1607–1615.
35. *United States Geological Survey Yearbook, Fiscal Year 1987*, p. 90.
36. Frank Trippett, "A Big Stink on the Pigeon," *Time*, June 6, 1988, p. 22.
37. Peter Von Stackelberg, "White Wash: the Dioxin Cover-up," *Greenpeace*, March/April 1989, pp. 7–11.
38. Mary Kadlecek, "Toxics in a Great River—Putting the Pieces Together," *The Conservationist*, November/December 1987, p. 39.
39. Office of Environmental Programs, Maryland Department of Health and Mental Hygiene, *Maryland Air and Water Quality Atlas*, 1986, p. 32.
40. Jerry Adler and Karen Springen, "Where Will the Cranes Go?" *Newsweek*, April 3, 1989, p. 62.

Chapter Seven: Seas of Debris

41. Kathryn O'Hara, "The Coastal Environment: Beaches." *EPA Journal*, September/October 1989, p. 25.
42. Michael R. Deland, "Boston Harbor: No Party After the Tea Party," *EPA Journal*, June 1988, pp. 24–26.
43. Betsy Carpenter, "Superfund, Superflop," *U.S. News & World Report*, February 6, 1989, p. 47.
44. Kathryn J. O'Hara, et al. *A Citizen's Guide to Plastics in the Ocean: More Than a Litter Problem.* (Washington, D.C.: Center for Environmental Education, 1988).
45. Ibid, p. 83.

46. J.B.C. Jackson, et al., "Ecological Effects of a Major Oil Spill on Panamanian Coastal Marine Communities," *Science*, January 6, 1989, pp. 37–43.
47. Edward Goldsmith and Nicholas Hildyard, eds. *The Earth Report*. (London: Mitchell Beazley Publishers; Los Angeles: Price Stern Sloan, 1988), pp. 185–186, 191–194.
48. "Should Sewage Sludge Be Dumped at Sea? A Point/Counterpoint," *EPA Journal*, June 1988, pp. 8–10.

Chapter Eight: When Wells, Rivers, and Lakes Go Dry

49. United States Department of Agriculture. *The Second RCA Appraisal Soil, Water, and Related Resources on Nonfederal Land in the United States Analysis of Condition and Trends*, Review Draft, July/August 1987, section 7, p. 1.
50. Marc Reisner, "The Emerald Desert," *Greenpeace*, July/August 1989, p. 6.
51. Donald R. Coates, *Geology and Society* (New York, London: Chapman and Hall, 1985), p. 78.

Chapter Nine: Protective Measures

52. Gro Harlem Brundtland, "Seeking Global Ethic," *EPA Journal*, July/August 1988, p. 24.
53. Gregg Easterbrook, "Cleaning Up Our Mess," *Newsweek*, July 24, 1989, p. 36.
54. "Farmers Speak," *EPA Journal*, April 1988, p. 14.
55. Charles E. Knox, "What's Going on Down There?" *Science News*, December 3, 1988, pp. 362–363.
56. Sharon Begley with Theresa Waldrop, "Microbes to the Rescue!" *Newsweek*, June 19, 1989, pp. 56–57.

Chapter Ten: Taking Action

57. Ginia Bellafante, "Bottled Water: Fads and Facts," *Garbage: The Practical Journal for the Environment*, January/February 1990, p. 48.

GLOSSARY

absorption—the process of taking one substance into another.

acidic—containing or forming an acid.

adsorption—attraction of chemical compounds to the surface of a solid.

aerobic—active only in the presence of oxygen.

agrochemicals—chemicals used to improve the quality and quantity of farm products.

algae—primitive plants having one or many cells and usually adapted to water.

alkaline—able to neutralize acids.

anaerobic—active in the absence of oxygen.

aquatic—of or adapted to water.

aquifer—an underground bed of permeable rock, sand, or gravel, that is a source of water.

bioremediation—a process in which microbes feed on various pollutants in water and soil.

carbon—an element that occurs in many chemical compounds.

carbon dioxide—an odorless, tasteless, and colorless gas that is part of air and is released from human beings and animals.

coagulation—a process of changing liquid to a semi-solid or solid mass.

decompose—to decay.

deicing—melting or freeing of ice.

dredging—scooping or digging soil from the bottom of a body of water.

ecology—the study of how living things relate to their environment.

effluent—the discharge of a pollutant.

erosion—the wearing away of rocks and soil particles.

estuary—area of a river near the sea where fresh water and seawater mix.

[136]

eutrophication—the natural or artificial process of enriching a waterbody so that it fills with aquatic plants and is low in oxygen.

evapotranspiration—the loss of water from soil and plant surfaces.

flotation—a process of allowing solids to float on a surface.

hydrocarbon—compounds of hydrogen and carbon found in oil, coal, and natural gas.

larvae—the juvenile or wormlike forms of insects and fish that hatch from eggs.

leaching—removal or escape of soluble materials from soil or from a container.

marine—of the seas or oceans.

nitrogen—a gas that makes up 78 percent of the atmosphere and is essential to all forms of life.

NOAA—National Oceanic and Atmospheric Administration.

oceanographer—a person who explores and studies the oceans.

pathogens—disease-causing organisms.

percolation—the movement of water or other liquids down through the soil.

photosynthesis—the process by which green plants use sunlight to produce energy from carbon dioxide and water.

phytoplankton—microscopic plants that drift in water and are the basis of the aquatic food chain.

plankton—the small plants and animals that live in or on the surfaces of oceans or bodies of fresh water.

potable—drinkable.

salinity—the salt content of a liquid or soil.

sediment—particles of solid matter that move from their original site to settle on a land surface or at the bottom of a waterway or body of water.

sludge—the solid part of sewage.

solvent—usually a liquid in which other substances dissolve.

TCE—trichloroethylene, an industrial solvent. Also an abbreviation for tetrachloroethylene.

tetrachloroethylene—an industrial solvent.

toluene—a solvent.

toxic—poisonous.

toxic plume—the emission or spread of hazardous materials discharged underground or into the air.

USDA—U.S. Department of Agriculture.

USGS—U.S. Geological Survey.

vinyl chloride—a chemical used in the manufacture of plastics and as a refrigerant.

watershed—an area in which all the water drains to a common elevation.

xylene—a chemical solvent.

[137]

FOR FURTHER READING

Books

Ashworth, William. *The Late, Great Lakes.* Detroit: Wayne State University Press, 1987.

Chicago Tribune staff. *Save Our Lake* (booklet). Chicago: The Chicago Tribune, 1967.

The Conservation Foundation. *Groundwater: Saving the Unseen Resource.* Washington, D.C.: The Conservation Foundation, 1987.

Gay, Kathlyn. *Acid Rain.* New York: Franklin Watts, 1983.

Gay, Kathlyn. *Silent Killers.* New York: Franklin Watts, 1988.

Goldin, Augusta. *Water. Too Much, Too Little, Too Polluted?* San Diego: Harcourt Brace Jovanovich, 1983.

Goldsmith, Edward, and Hildyard, Nicholas. *The Earth Report.* London: Mitchell Beazley Publishers, 1988; Los Angeles: Price Stern Sloan, 1988.

Lambert, David. *The Superbook of Our Planet.* New York: Willowisp Press, 1986.

Lefkowitz, R. J. *Save It! Keep It! Use It Again!* New York: Parents' Magazine Press, 1977

O'Hara, Kathryn J., et al. *A Citizen's Guide to Plastics in the Ocean: More Than a Litter Problem.* Washington, D.C.: Center for Marine Conservation, 1988.

Pringle, Laurence. *Restoring Our Earth.* Hillside, N.J.: Enslow Publishers, 1987.

Pringle, Laurence. *Water: The Next Resource Battle.* New York: Macmillan Publishing, 1982; London: Collier Macmillan, 1982.

Sedge, Michael H. *Commercialization of the Oceans.* New York: Franklin Watts, 1987.

Seymour, John, and Herbert Girardet. *Blueprint for a Green Planet.* New York: Prentice Hall Press, 1987; London: Dorling Kindersley Ltd., 1987.

[138]

Weber, Michael, et al. *The 1985 Citizen's Guide to the Ocean.* Washington, D.C. Center for Marine Conservation, 1985.

Periodicals

Adler, Jerry, with Springen, Karen. "Where Will the Cranes Go?" *Newsweek*, April 3, 1989, pp. 62–63.

Begley, Sharon, with Drew, Lisa, and Hager, Mary. "Smothering the Waters." *Newsweek*, April 10, 1989, pp. 54–57.

Bellafante, Ginia. "Bottled Water: Fads and Facts." *Garbage: The Practical Journal for the Environment*, January/February 1990, pp. 46–50.

Castleman, Michael. "Is Your Water Safe to Drink?" *Redbook*, July 1988, pp. 90–91, 128–130.

Cole, Tim. "Oceans on the Brink." *Popular Mechanics*, December 1987, p. 42.

Conner, Daniel Deith, and O'Dell, Robert. "The Tightening Net of Marine Plastics Pollution." *Environment*, January/February 1988, pp. 16–36.

"Don't Go Near the Water" (special report). *Newsweek*, August 1, 1988, pp. 42–48.

Easterbrook, Gregg. "Cleaning Up Our Mess." *Newsweek*, July 24, 1989, pp. 26–42.

"First Volleys of New Water Wars." *U.S. News & World Report*, May 30, 1988, pp. 20–22.

Forslund, Janne. "Quality Groundwater for Tomorrow." *World Health*, December 1986, pp. 25–26.

Fruhling, Larry. "Please Don't Drink the Water." *The Progressive*, October 1986, pp. 31–33.

"Fungi: California's Answer to Selenium?" *Science News*, July 4, 1987, p. 8.

Hudson, Marc. "Warning: The Friday Night Fish Fry May Be Hazardous to Your Health." *Audubon*, July 1987, pp. 24–41.

Kaplan, Justine. "The Not-So-Great Lakes." *Omni*, February 1989, p. 32.

Kay, Roger L. "Please Do Drink the Water." *World Monitor*, April 1989, pp. 20–22.

Knox, Charles E. "What's Going on Down There?" *Science News*, December 3, 1988, pp. 362–365.

Laycock, George. "What Water for Stillwater?" *Audubon*, November 1988, pp. 14–25.

Marinelli, Janet. "After the Flush." *Garbage: The Practical Journal for the Environment*, January/February 1990, pp. 24–35.

Marx, Wesley. "Swamped by Our Own Sewage." *Reader's Digest*, January 1988, pp. 123–128.

McCarthy, Abigail. "Global Peril, Local Action." *Commonweal*, October 7, 1988, pp. 520–521.

McKay, Bruce. "Fish Story." *Greenpeace*, July/August 1989, pp. 12–13.

Millemann, Beth. "Wretched Refuse off Our Shores." *Sierra*, January/February 1989, pp. 26–28.

"1988 Environment" (special report). *Discover*, January 1989, pp. 30–36.

"Planet of the Year" (special report). *Time*, January 2, 1989, pp. 24–73.

Reisner, Marc. "The Emerald Desert." *Greenpeace*, July/August 1989, pp. 6–10.

Riley, Michael. "Dead Cats, Toxins and Typhoid." *Time*, April 20, 1987, p. 69.

Roberts, Leslie. "A Corrosive Fight Over California's Toxics Law." *Science*, January 20, 1989, pp. 306–309.

St. Onge, Julie. "Runoff Runs Amok." *Sierra*, November/December 1988, pp. 28–32.

Satchell, Michael. "Where Have All the Ducks Gone?" *U.S. News & World Report*, October 24, 1988, p. 72.

Smith, Richard A.; Alexander, Richard B.; and Wolman, M. Gordon. "Water-Quality Trends in the Nation's Rivers." *Science*, March 27, 1987, pp. 1607–1615.

Stamps, David. "The Real Price of Road Salt." *National Wildlife*, December/January 1989, p. 28.

Stayton, Robert. "Sludge Busters." *Popular Science*, February 1987, pp. 43–44.

Stearns, Bob. "Troubled Times for the Tarpon." *Field and Stream*, November 1987, pp. 80–81.

Sun, Marjorie. "Ground Water Ills: Many Diagnoses, Few Remedies." *Science*, June 20, 1986, pp. 1490–1493.

Toufexis, Anastasia. "The Dirty Seas." *Time*, August 1, 1988, pp. 44–50.

Trippett, Frank. "A Big Stink on the Pigeon." *Time*, June 6, 1988, p. 22.

Weisskopf, Michael. "Plastic Reaps a Grim Harvest in the Oceans of the World." *Smithsonian*, March 1988, pp. 59–66.

Young, Helen. "New PCB Alert." *Good Housekeeping*, April 1988, p. 255.

NOTE: In honor of Earth Day, April 22, 1990, many nationally distributed magazines published from January to April 1990 carried articles on how individuals could take action to protect water and other environmental resources.

INDEX

Acid shock, 72
Acidic lakes, 70–73
Acidic rivers, 80
Adsorption, 21
Aerobic bacteria, 40, 42
Agencies and organizations, 130–131
Agricultural contaminants, 30–33, 118–119
Agrochemicals, 64, 74
Algae, 15, 88
Anaerobic bacteria, 40
Aquifers, 10–11, 19–20, 27, 30, 51–52, 110
  contamination, 20–23
  overuse, 35–36
Ashworth, William, 15
Attack bugs, 119–120

Beaches, 86–89
  raw sewage, 15–16
Biocontrol, 119
Bioremediation, 119–120
Birth defects, 23
Biscayne Aquifer, 51–52
Blowout, 95, 96
Blue-baby syndrome, 23
BOD, 39
Brundtland, Gro Harlem, 113
Bureau of Reclamation, 104, 108

Cancer, 23, 24
Cesspools, 23
Circular system of water use, 44–45
Cleanup methods, 119–121
CMC, 86, 92, 94
Coagulation, 40
Coates, Donald, 110
Conservation Reserve Program, 111
Consumption, water, 13–14

Dams, 13, 82–83, 103, 104, 107
DEC, 78–79
Deicing salt, 33
Dioxin, 67, 78
Diseases, waterborne, 24
Dolphins, 84, 86, 91–92
Doxtater, Gary, 61
Dredgings, 98
Drinking water, 9, 18, 125–127
  Italy, 30
  suggestions, 127–129
  West Germany, 30
Dual water systems, 43
Duck factories, 49
Duck Stamps, 58
Dumps, 29–30

Easterbrook, Gregg, 117

141

Education, 122–124, 125
Effluents, 81
Environmental laws, 113–115, 117
EPA, 14, 24, 30, 39, 48, 52, 59, 81, 87, 117, 126
  groundwater, 18, 27, 114
  lakes, 60, 63, 64, 65, 73
  PCB's, 86, 101
  underground tanks, 28–29
Erosion, 81
Estuary, 41, 42
Eutrophic, 15, 60
Eutrophication, 15, 39, 45, 64, 114
Evaportranspiration, 11
Everglades, 48, 51–52

Farm runoff, 32
Farmers, 32, 64, 109–111, 119
Fertilizers, 30–31, 64
Flood control, 51
Flotation, 40
Fresh water
  percent available, 10
  pollutants, 14–17
  unequal distribution, 13–14
  worldwide supply, 11
  See also Water Resources

Geraci, Joseph, 84
Glass, Gary, 73
Great Dismal Swamp, 57
Great Lakes, 9, 16, 65–70
Greenpeace, 78, 86
Groundwater, 19–36, 111, 114
  agricultural contaminants, 30–33
  aquifer contamination, 20–23
  industrial wastes, 25–29
  landfills and dumps, 20–30
  overdrafts, 35–36

sewage, 23–25
urban pollutants, 33–35

Habitat stamp programs, 58
Hazardous wastes, 29, 33–35, 98–101
Human waste, 9, 15–16, 23–25
Hyacinths, 43–44
Hydrologic cycle, 11–12
Hypereutrophic, 15, 63

Improvements, 17–18
Indiana Harbor Ship Canal, 67
Industrial wastes, 25–29, 121–122
Integrated pest management, 118–119
Irrigation water, 14
IWLA, 56–57

Johnson, Lyndon B., 114

Kean, Thomas, 100
Koch, Edward, 100

Lakes, 60–73
  acidity, 70–73
  problems, 61–64
Landfills, 29–30
LDC, 98–99
Leaching, 24
Lineal system of water intake, 44
Love Canal, 29

MARPOL, 94
MDNR, 25, 27
Medical debris, 86

NASA, 44
NCP, 115, 118
Nebraska Rainwater Basin, 48
New River, 74
Nitrates, 23, 24, 126

Nitrogen, 15
NOAA, 84, 92
Nutrient overload, 15–16

O'Hara, Kathryn, 86
Ocean dumping, 98–101
Ocean Dumping Act, 99
Ocean incineration, 98–101
Oil, 9, 95–98
Outhouses, 23
Overdrafts, 35–36

Pathogens, 16, 23–24, 30, 60
PCBs, 65–67, 77–80, 84, 86,
    87, 101
Percolation, 21
Pesticides, 30–32, 52, 66–67,
    82, 117, 118
Phosphorus, 15
Photosynthesis, 123
Pigeon River, 77
Plankton, 66
Plastics, 89, 91–94
Pocosins, 48
Pollutants, 14–17
    control of, 17–18
Pollution examples, 74–75
Population, increase, 10
Protective measures, 112–124
    attack bugs, 119–120
    cleanup methods,
        119–120
    controlling toxins,
        121–122
    cooperative efforts,
        117–119
    education, 122–124
    environmental laws,
        113–115, 117

Radon, 23
Raw sewage, 15–16, 39
Reagan, Ronald, 17
Reclamation projects, 43–45
Recycling, plastic, 94

Recycling, water, 42–43
Red tides, 84
Reisner, Marc, 109
Rivers, 39, 74–83
    industrial wastes, 16
    water quality, 75–77

Salinity, 10
Salinization, 103
Seas, 84–101
Sediment, 61, 88
Sedimentation tank, 40
Selenium, 32–33
Septic tanks, 23, 24–25
Sewage, 23–25, 39, 98–101
Sewer systems, 37–38
Sheaffer, John, 44
Shellfish, 50
Silicon Valley, 28
Simmons, Harold, 107
Sinking land, 35, 102
Sludge, 40, 99–100
Soil Conservation Service, 59
Swamp. See Wetlands
Swampbuster provisions, 58

Tertiary treatment, 42
Thomas Pell Wildlife
    Sanctuary, 56
Toxic chemicals, 9, 75
Toxic plume, 20, 27
Toxic Substances Control Act,
    115
Toxins, controlling, 121–122

Underground storage tanks,
    28–29
Urban pollutants, 33–35
USDA, 13, 32, 58, 62
USGS, 24, 70, 76
U.S. Safe Drinking Water
    Act, 114

Waste water, 37–45
    disposal, 38–40

Waste water (*continued*)
   reclamation projects,
     43–45
   recycling, 42–43
   treating, 40–42
Water distribution, 13–14
Water quality, 75–77, 125–127
   measurement for, 38–39
   tips, 127–128
Water Quality Act, 114
Water reclamation, 42–43
Water resources, 10–11
   going dry, 102–111

   managing, 103–104
   obstacles to conservation,
     108–111
   stretching, 104–108
Water table, 19
Watershed, 31, 61
Wells, 24, 25, 26, 27–28
Wetland Watch, 57
Wetlands, 46–59, 83
   benefits, 49–52
   conservation, 54–59
   location, 48–49
   losses, 52–54
Wetlands Protection Act, 57